Cryptocurrency for Beginners, A Guidebook.

MG Horizon Editions

Table of Contents

Chapter 1:
Introduction to Cryptocurrency

What is Cryptocurrency?

Cryptocurrency, also known as digital currency, is a form of virtual or digital money that utilizes cryptographic technology to secure and verify transactions. Unlike traditional fiat currencies issued by central banks, cryptocurrencies operate independently of any central authority. They are decentralized, meaning they are not controlled or regulated by a government or financial institution.

At the core of cryptocurrencies is the concept of blockchain, a distributed ledger technology that records and verifies transactions across a network of computers. This technology ensures transparency, security, and immutability of transactions. Each transaction is encrypted and linked to the previous transaction, forming a chain of blocks, hence the name "blockchain."

One of the defining features of cryptocurrencies is their digital nature. They exist solely in electronic form and are not physical coins or banknotes. Instead, they are represented by unique strings of code stored on digital wallets. These wallets can be software-based, such as mobile or desktop applications, or hardware devices specifically designed for securely storing cryptocurrencies.

Cryptocurrencies provide several advantages over traditional forms of currency. Firstly, they offer increased security with cryptographic algorithms that protect against counterfeiting and fraud. Transactions are conducted using public and private key pairs, ensuring that only the owner of the cryptocurrency can initiate transfers.

Another key advantage is the potential for increased privacy. While transactions made with cryptocurrencies are recorded on the blockchain and are visible to all participants, the identities of the individuals involved are typically pseudonymous. This allows users to maintain a certain level of privacy and control over their financial transactions.

Cryptocurrencies also offer the potential for fast and efficient global transactions. Traditional cross-border transactions can be slow, expensive, and subject to intermediaries. With cryptocurrencies, transactions can be conducted directly between parties across the globe, bypassing the need for intermediaries and reducing transaction fees and settlement times. However, cryptocurrencies also come with certain risks and challenges. One of the primary concerns is their volatility. Cryptocurrency prices can fluctuate dramatically within short periods, making them subject to high levels of speculation and investment risk. Additionally, the regulatory landscape surrounding cryptocurrencies is still evolving, and there are concerns regarding consumer protection, money laundering, and tax compliance.

Understanding the fundamentals of cryptocurrency is crucial for beginners entering the space. By grasping the concept of decentralized digital money and its underlying technology, individuals can navigate the world of cryptocurrencies more confidently and make informed decisions regarding their use and investment.

A Brief History of Cryptocurrencies

The history of cryptocurrencies can be traced back to the emergence of Bitcoin, the world's first decentralized digital currency. In 2008, an anonymous individual or group of individuals using the pseudonym Satoshi Nakamoto published a white-paper titled "Bitcoin: A Peer-to-Peer Electronic Cash System." This whitepaper laid the foundation for the development of Bitcoin and introduced the concept of a decentralized, trustless digital currency.

In January 2009, the Bitcoin network went live, and the first block, known as the genesis block, was mined. This marked the beginning of a new era in finance and technology. Bitcoin's underlying technology, the blockchain, allowed for the secure and transparent recording of transactions on a distributed network of computers.

The early years of Bitcoin were characterized by a small community of enthusiasts and developers experimenting with the technology. In the early days, Bitcoin had little to no monetary value, and its adoption was limited to a niche audience. However, as more people became aware of its potential, interest in Bitcoin began to grow.

In 2010, the first documented real-world transaction involving Bitcoin took place when Laszlo Hanyecz famously purchased two pizzas for 10,000 bitcoins. This event is now celebrated as Bitcoin Pizza Day and is considered a milestone in the history of cryptocurrencies.

Bitcoin's popularity continued to increase, and in 2011, alternative cryptocurrencies, often referred to as altcoins, started to emerge. These altcoins aimed to address certain limitations or introduce new features not present in Bitcoin. Examples of early altcoins include Litecoin, Namecoin, and Ripple.

The year 2013 marked a significant milestone for cryptocurrencies as Bitcoin experienced its first major price rally. The value of Bitcoin reached over $1,000 for the first time, capturing global media attention, and attracting a broader audience to the world of cryptocurrencies.

In the following years, the cryptocurrency market expanded rapidly, with the introduction of various innovative projects and technologies. Ethereum, launched in 2015, brought smart contracts and decentralized applications (DApps) to the forefront. This opened new possibilities for developers to build decentralized applications on the blockchain.

The year 2017 saw an unprecedented surge in the cryptocurrency market, with Bitcoin reaching its all-time high near $20,000. This bull run was followed by a significant market correction in 2018, highlighting the volatility and speculative nature of the cryptocurrency market.

Since then, cryptocurrencies have continued to evolve and gain mainstream recognition. Major financial institutions and corporations have started to explore blockchain technology and cryptocurrencies, recognizing their potential for efficiency, transparency, and financial inclusion.

The regulatory landscape surrounding cryptocurrencies has also undergone significant changes. Governments and regulatory bodies have been grappling with how to approach and regulate cryptocurrencies, with some countries embracing them as a legitimate form of currency and others imposing restrictions and regulations.

Today, cryptocurrencies have become a global phenomenon, with thousands of different cryptocurrencies in existence, each with its own unique features and use cases. The technology behind cryptocurrencies, blockchain, has also found applications in various industries beyond finance, including supply chain management, healthcare, and voting systems.

The brief history of cryptocurrencies demonstrates the transformative potential of decentralized digital currencies and their underlying blockchain technology. It has paved the way for a new financial paradigm, offering individuals greater control over their financial assets and opening opportunities for innovation and disruption in multiple sectors.

The Inner Workings of Cryptocurrencies

Cryptocurrencies operate on the principles of blockchain technology, which forms the backbone of their functionality and security. Understanding the inner workings of cryptocurrencies involves delving into key components such as blockchain, mining, consensus mechanisms, and digital wallets.

Blockchain Technology: At the heart of cryptocurrencies lies the concept of blockchain, a decentralized and distributed ledger that records and verifies transactions. A blockchain consists of a chain of blocks, with each block containing a set of transactions. The blocks are linked together using cryptographic hashes, forming an immutable and transparent record of all transactions within the network. This distributed nature of blockchain ensures that no single entity has control over the entire network, making it resistant to tampering and censorship.

Mining: Mining is the process by which new cryptocurrency coins or tokens are created and transactions are verified within a blockchain network. Miners, using powerful computers, compete to solve complex mathematical puzzles. The first miner to solve the puzzle adds a new block to the blockchain and is rewarded with a predetermined amount of cryptocurrency. Mining serves two primary purposes: verifying the validity of transactions and securing the network through the use of computational power.

Consensus Mechanisms: Consensus mechanisms are protocols employed by blockchain networks to ensure agreement among participants on the state of the blockchain and the validity of transactions. The most widely known consensus mechanism is Proof of Work (PoW), used by Bitcoin and many other cryptocurrencies. PoW requires miners to solve computationally intensive puzzles to validate transactions and secure the network.

Other consensus mechanisms such as Proof of Stake (PoS) and Delegated Proof of Stake (DPoS), offer alternative approaches that require participants to hold or lock up a certain amount of cryptocurrency to participate in block validation and consensus.

Digital Wallets: Digital wallets are software or hardware-based tools that store the public and private keys necessary to access and manage cryptocurrencies. A public key serves as an address to receive funds, while a private key is a secret code that allows users to access and authorize transactions from their wallet. Digital wallets can be divided into two main types: hot wallets and cold wallets. Hot wallets are connected to the internet and offer convenience but may be more susceptible to hacking. Cold wallets, on the other hand, store keys offline, providing enhanced security but requiring additional steps for transaction authorization.

Together, these components form the intricate workings of cryptocurrencies. The decentralized nature of blockchain, coupled with mining and consensus mechanisms, ensures the security, transparency, and integrity of cryptocurrency transactions. Digital wallets enable users to securely store and manage their cryptocurrency holdings, providing access to this new form of digital wealth. Understanding these inner workings is essential for individuals seeking to engage with cryptocurrencies safely and confidently.

Advantages of Cryptocurrency

Cryptocurrencies offer a range of advantages over traditional forms of currency and financial systems. Understanding these advantages is crucial for anyone considering the use or investment in cryptocurrencies. Here are some key benefits:

1. Security: Cryptocurrencies employ advanced cryptographic techniques to secure transactions and control the creation of new units. The decentralized nature of cryptocurrencies, combined with the use of public and private key encryption, ensures that transactions are secure and resistant to fraud and hacking. This increased security can provide individuals with greater confidence in conducting digital transactions and storing their wealth.

2. Privacy: While cryptocurrencies operate on public blockchains, they often provide a certain degree of privacy and pseudonymity. Transactions made with cryptocurrencies are typically linked to wallet addresses rather than personal identities. This can protect users' privacy and prevent third parties from accessing their financial information without their consent.

3. Accessibility: Cryptocurrencies have the potential to provide financial services to individuals who may not have access to traditional banking systems. With just an internet connection, anyone can create a cryptocurrency wallet and participate in global financial transactions. This inclusivity can empower individuals in underbanked or poor regions, facilitating financial independence and economic growth.

4. Global Transactions: Traditional cross-border transactions can be expensive, time-consuming, and subject to intermediaries such as banks and remittance services. Cryptocurrencies enable fast, low-cost, peer-to-peer transactions across borders, bypassing the need for intermediaries. This can greatly simplify and expedite international transactions, facilitating global trade and remittances.

5. Financial Control: Cryptocurrencies give users direct control over their funds without relying on third-party institutions. Users have sole ownership and access to their private keys, allowing them to manage and transfer their funds at their own discretion. This decentralized control aligns with the principles of financial sovereignty and empowers individuals to oversee their own financial destinies.

6. Transparency: The use of blockchain technology in cryptocurrencies ensures transparency and immutability of transactions. All transactions recorded on the blockchain are visible to participants, creating a transparent and auditable financial system. This transparency can help combat fraud, corruption, and money laundering by making transactions traceable and publicly accountable.

7. Innovation and Disruption: Cryptocurrencies have sparked a wave of innovation and disruptive potential across various industries. The underlying technology, blockchain, has applications beyond financial transactions, including supply chain management, healthcare, voting systems, and more. This innovation and disruption have the potential to reshape industries and create new opportunities for economic growth and efficiency.

While cryptocurrencies offer numerous advantages, it is important to acknowledge that they also come with certain risks and challenges. Volatility, regulatory uncertainty, and security vulnerabilities are factors that users and investors should be aware of and take into consideration. However, when used responsibly and with proper precautions, cryptocurrencies can provide individuals with new financial opportunities and empower them to participate in the digital economy.

Potential Risks and Challenges

While cryptocurrencies offer several advantages, it's important to be aware of the potential risks and challenges associated with their use. Understanding these factors can help individuals make informed decisions and take appropriate precautions. Here are some key considerations:

1. Volatility: Cryptocurrencies are known for their price volatility. The value of cryptocurrencies can experience significant fluctuations within short periods. This volatility can result in substantial gains or losses for investors. It is important to approach cryptocurrency investments with caution and be prepared for price swings.

2. Regulatory Uncertainty: The regulatory landscape surrounding cryptocurrencies is still evolving in many jurisdictions. Governments and regulatory bodies are grappling with how to address cryptocurrencies and may introduce new regulations and policies that can impact their use, taxation, and legality. Changes in regulations can influence the value and accessibility of cryptocurrencies.

3. Security Risks: While cryptocurrencies use advanced cryptographic techniques for security, they are not immune to security risks. Cyber-attacks, hacking attempts, and phishing scams can pose threats to cryptocurrency holders. It is crucial to employ strong security measures, such as using reputable wallets, enabling two-factor authentication, and being cautious of suspicious links or requests for personal information.

4. Market Manipulation and Scams: The cryptocurrency market can be susceptible to manipulation and fraudulent activities. Pump-and-dump schemes, fake initial coin offerings (ICOs), and fraudulent exchanges are risks that investors should be aware of. Conducting thorough research, verifying the credibility of projects, and exercising caution when investing or trading can help mitigate these risks.

5. Irreversible Transactions: Transactions made with cryptocurrencies are typically irreversible. Once a transaction is confirmed on the blockchain, it cannot be easily reversed or canceled. This can be advantageous for security but also means that caution must be exercised to ensure accurate transaction details and trusted recipients.

6. User Error and Loss of Funds: The responsibility of managing and securing cryptocurrency funds rests with the individual user. User error, such as forgetting wallet passwords or losing private keys, can result in permanent loss of access to funds. It is essential to follow best practices for wallet security, including regular backups and secure storage of private keys.

7. Scalability and Technology Limitations: Blockchain technology, while innovative, still faces scalability and technological limitations. The transaction processing speed and capacity of certain cryptocurrencies may be limited, leading to delays and higher fees during periods of high network activity. Additionally, the energy consumption associated with some cryptocurrencies, particularly those using proof-of-work consensus mechanisms, is a concern in terms of environmental impact.

 By understanding and addressing these risks and challenges, individuals can navigate the cryptocurrency landscape more effectively and make informed decisions. It is advisable to stay updated on industry developments, follow best security practices, conduct due diligence, and seek professional advice when necessary. Responsible participation in the cryptocurrency ecosystem can help mitigate potential risks and maximize the benefits offered by this emerging technology.

Getting Started with Cryptocurrencies

   Entering the world of cryptocurrencies can be both exciting and overwhelming, especially for beginners. Here are some essential steps to help you get started:

1. **Educate Yourself:** Begin by educating yourself about cryptocurrencies, blockchain technology, and the underlying concepts. Read books, articles, and reputable online resources to gain a solid understanding of how cryptocurrencies work, their potential benefits, and the associated risks.

2. **Determine Your Goals:** Define your objectives for getting involved with cryptocurrencies. Are you interested in investing, using cryptocurrencies for transactions, or exploring blockchain technology? Clarifying your goals will help you make informed decisions and stay focused on what you want to achieve.

3. **Choose a Reliable Exchange:** To buy and sell cryptocurrencies, you'll need to choose a reputable cryptocurrency exchange. Research and compare different exchanges based on factors such as security, user experience, available cryptocurrencies, fees, and customer support. Consider using well-established exchanges with a good track record.

4. **Set Up a Wallet:** Select a digital wallet to securely store your cryptocurrencies. Wallets can be software-based (mobile, desktop, or web) or hardware devices. Hardware wallets, such as Ledger or Trezor, offer enhanced security as they store your private keys offline. Follow the instructions provided by the wallet provider to set up your wallet and ensure you back up your recovery phrase securely.

5. **Complete the Verification Process:** On most cryptocurrency exchanges, you'll need to complete a verification process before you can start trading. This process typically involves providing identification documents and verifying your personal information. Follow the exchange's instructions carefully to complete the verification process.

6. **Start with a Small Investment:** If you're interested in investing in cryptocurrencies, start with a small amount that you can afford to lose. Cryptocurrency prices can be volatile, and it's important to approach investments with a long-term perspective. Consider diversifying your investment across different cryptocurrencies to mitigate risk.

7. **Stay Informed:** Keep up with the latest news, developments, and market trends in the cryptocurrency space. Follow reliable sources, join cryptocurrency communities, and engage in discussions to stay informed. This will help you make better decisions and adapt to the evolving landscape.

8. **Practice Security Measures:** Protect your cryptocurrencies by implementing strong security measures. Use unique and complex passwords, enable two-factor authentication, and be cautious of phishing attempts. Regularly update your software wallets and keep your hardware wallets in a secure location.

9. **Learn from Experience:** As you gain experience with cryptocurrencies, learn from both successes and setbacks. Reflect on your investment decisions, analyze market trends, and adjust your strategies accordingly. Continuous learning and adapting to the dynamic nature of cryptocurrencies will help you navigate the space effectively.

Remember, the world of cryptocurrencies is constantly evolving, and it's important to stay informed and adapt to changes. Be patient, take calculated risks, and approach cryptocurrencies with a long-term perspective. With proper knowledge, security measures, and a thoughtful approach, you can embark on your cryptocurrency journey confidently.

The Future of Cryptocurrencies

The future of cryptocurrencies holds immense potential for further growth, innovation, and adoption. Here are some key trends and developments that could shape the future of this exciting industry:

1. **Mainstream Adoption:** Cryptocurrencies have been gradually gaining mainstream acceptance, with increasing recognition from governments, financial institutions, and corporations. As regulatory frameworks become clearer and institutional infrastructure continues to develop, cryptocurrencies may become more integrated into traditional financial systems, potentially leading to wider adoption and increased use cases.

2. **Central Bank Digital Currencies (CBDCs):** Central banks worldwide are exploring the concept of issuing their own digital currencies known as CBDCs. CBDCs aim to provide a digital representation of a country's fiat currency and are backed by the central bank. The introduction of CBDCs could potentially bridge the gap between traditional fiat currencies and cryptocurrencies, offering a government-sanctioned digital currency that combines the benefits of cryptocurrencies with regulatory oversight.

3. **Enhanced Scalability and Interoperability:** Scalability has been a significant challenge for many cryptocurrencies, leading to congestion and high transaction fees during periods of high demand. However, ongoing research and development efforts are focused on improving scalability and interoperability within blockchain networks. Solutions such as layer-2 protocols, sharding, and cross-chain interoperability projects aim to address these limitations, enabling faster and more efficient transactions across multiple blockchains.

4. **Decentralized Finance (DeFi):** DeFi has emerged as a prominent sector within the cryptocurrency industry, providing decentralized alternatives to traditional financial services such as lending, borrowing, and trading. DeFi protocols built on blockchain networks enable permissionless access to financial services, removing intermediaries and offering greater financial inclusivity. The growth of DeFi has been remarkable, with increasing adoption, innovative products, and significant investments flowing into the sector.

5. **Tokenization of Assets:** The tokenization of real-world assets, including real estate, art, and commodities, has gained traction in recent years. By representing these assets as digital tokens on a blockchain, tokenization enhances liquidity, fractional ownership, and accessibility. Tokenization has the potential to democratize investing, allowing individuals to gain exposure to previously illiquid or inaccessible assets.

6. **Improved User Experience:** As the cryptocurrency industry matures, user experience (UX) and user interface (UI) design are becoming more user-friendly and intuitive. Efforts are being made to simplify the onboarding process, enhance security measures, and provide seamless experiences for users interacting with cryptocurrencies and blockchain applications. User-friendly wallets, decentralized applications (DApps), and intuitive platforms aim to make cryptocurrency adoption more accessible to a wider audience.

7. **Environmental Sustainability:** The environmental impact of cryptocurrencies, particularly those using proof-of-work consensus mechanisms, has drawn attention. As sustainability becomes a more pressing concern, the industry is actively exploring alternative consensus mechanisms and energy-efficient protocols.

Projects adopting proof-of-stake (PoS), proof-of-authority (PoA), and other energy-efficient approaches aim to reduce the carbon footprint associated with cryptocurrency mining.

The future of cryptocurrencies is dynamic and subject to various factors, including technological advancements, regulatory developments, and market dynamics. While uncertainties and challenges persist, the continued growth and innovation in the cryptocurrency space suggest that cryptocurrencies will likely play an increasingly significant role in our financial systems, economy, and daily lives. It's an exciting time to be a part of this transformative industry and staying informed and adaptable will be key to navigating the future of cryptocurrencies successfully.

Chapter 2:
Understanding Blockchain Technology

What is Blockchain?

Blockchain is a revolutionary technology that serves as the foundation for cryptocurrencies like Bitcoin, but its potential extends far beyond digital currencies. At its core, a blockchain is a decentralized, immutable, and transparent ledger that records and verifies transactions across a network of computers.

A blockchain consists of a chain of blocks, where each block contains a list of transactions. These transactions can represent the transfer of digital assets, ownership records, or any other form of information that can be stored digitally. The blocks are linked to each other in a chronological order, forming a chain, hence the name "blockchain."

The defining characteristic of blockchain technology is its decentralized nature. Unlike traditional centralized systems where a single authority controls the ledger, a blockchain is maintained and validated by a distributed network of participants known as nodes. Each node has a copy of the entire blockchain and independently verifies the transactions to ensure consensus on the state of the ledger.

To ensure the security and integrity of the blockchain, transactions are bundled together into blocks and cryptographically secured using hash functions. Hash functions convert the data within a block into a fixed-length string of characters known as a hash. These hashes are unique and act as digital fingerprints for the data. Any change in the data, no matter how small, will result in a completely different hash, alerting the network to the tampering attempt.

Additionally, each block contains a reference to the previous block's hash, effectively creating a link between blocks. This linking mechanism ensures the immutability of the blockchain. Once a block is added to the chain, it becomes extremely difficult to alter or remove, as it would require changing the hash of that block and all subsequent blocks in the chain. This property provides transparency and trust, as the entire history of transactions can be audited and verified.

Another essential aspect of blockchain technology is its transparency. As a distributed ledger, the blockchain allows all participants to view and validate the transactions stored on the network. This transparency promotes trust among participants and reduces the need for intermediaries or third-party verification.

While originally developed for cryptocurrencies, blockchain technology has gained recognition for its potential applications in various industries. Its decentralized and transparent nature offers advantages in sectors such as supply chain management, finance, healthcare, voting systems, identity verification, intellectual property protection, and more. By eliminating the need for intermediaries and enabling secure and efficient data transfer, blockchain has the potential to streamline processes, reduce fraud, and increase trust in numerous domains.

Understanding the fundamentals of blockchain technology is essential for grasping the potential benefits and challenges associated with cryptocurrencies and exploring the broader applications of this transformative technology in the upcoming chapters.

Cryptographic Hash Functions

Cryptographic hash functions play a crucial role in blockchain technology by ensuring the integrity and security of the data stored within blocks. Let's explore the key characteristics and functions of cryptographic hash functions.

A cryptographic hash function is a mathematical algorithm that takes an input (data) of any size and produces a fixed-length string of characters, typically represented as a hash or digest. This output has a predetermined length, regardless of the size of the input data. Some commonly used cryptographic hash functions include SHA-256 (Secure Hash Algorithm 256-bit), SHA-3, and MD5 (Message Digest Algorithm 5).

Here are the key properties of cryptographic hash functions:

1. Deterministic: A given input will always produce the same hash output. This property ensures consistency and reliability in the hash generation process.

2. Quick Computation: Hash functions are designed to compute the hash of an input quickly, regardless of the size of the input data. This efficiency is crucial for processing large volumes of transactions within a blockchain network.

3. Preimage Resistance: It should be computationally infeasible to determine the original input data from its hash. In other words, given a hash output, it should be extremely difficult (ideally impossible) to reverse-engineer the original data.

4. Collision Resistance: A collision occurs when two different inputs produce the same hash output. Cryptographic hash functions aim to minimize the likelihood of collisions, making it highly improbable for two different inputs to result in the same hash. Collision resistance ensures the uniqueness of each hash, strengthening the security of the blockchain.

5. Avalanche Effect: Even a slight change in the input data should produce a significantly different hash output. This property ensures that a small alteration in the input data will cause the resulting hash to appear completely different, preventing tampering or manipulation of the data.

Cryptographic hash functions have various applications within blockchain technology:

Data Integrity: Hash functions are used to verify the integrity of data stored within a block. By computing the hash of the data and storing it within the block, any modification to the data will result in a different hash, alerting the network to tampering attempts.

Block Verification: Each block in the blockchain contains a reference to the hash of the previous block. This linking mechanism ensures the integrity of the entire chain. If a previous block is tampered with, its hash will change, and the subsequent blocks' references will become invalid, preserving the immutability and integrity of the blockchain.

Digital Signatures: Cryptographic hash functions are used in digital signature schemes to ensure the authenticity and integrity of digital documents. By hashing the document and encrypting the hash with the private key of the signer, a digital signature is created. Verifying the signature involves decrypting the signature with the signer's public key, hashing the document, and comparing the two hashes.

Password Storage: Cryptographic hash functions are commonly used to store passwords securely. Instead of storing the actual passwords, a hash of the password is stored. When a user attempts to log in, the entered password is hashed and compared to the stored hash. This way, even if the password database is compromised, the original passwords are not easily revealed.

Cryptographic hash functions are a critical component of blockchain technology, providing data integrity, security, and verification mechanisms. Understanding their properties and applications is essential for comprehending the underlying security measures within a blockchain network.

Merkle Trees: Merkle trees, also known as hash trees, are data structures used to efficiently verify the integrity and inclusion of transactions within a block. Merkle trees allow for faster verification of large sets of data by condensing them into a single hash, known as the Merkle root. This Merkle root represents the entire set of transactions within a block.

Key Concepts of Blockchain

In this section, we will explore four key concepts of blockchain technology: decentralization, consensus mechanisms, immutable ledger, and smart contracts.

Decentralization

Decentralization is a fundamental principle of blockchain technology. Unlike traditional centralized systems where a single entity or authority has control over the network, blockchain operates in a decentralized manner. In a decentralized blockchain, the power and decision-making authority are distributed among a network of participants known as nodes.

Decentralization offers several advantages:

• Enhanced Security: With no single point of failure, decentralized blockchains are more resistant to hacking, censorship, and data manipulation. Each participant holds a copy of the blockchain, ensuring that a consensus must be reached among multiple nodes to validate transactions.

Transparency and Trust: Decentralization promotes transparency as each participant can view and verify the transactions stored on the blockchain. transparency builds trust among participants, as they can independently audit and validate the integrity of the system.

• Reducing Intermediaries: By eliminating intermediaries, decentralized blockchain networks can facilitate peer-to-peer transactions, removing the need for costly intermediaries such as banks or payment processors. This can lead to more efficient and cost-effective transactions.

Consensus Mechanisms

Consensus mechanisms are protocols that enable participants in a blockchain network to agree on the state of the blockchain and validate transactions. These mechanisms ensure that all nodes in the network reach a consensus on the validity and order of transactions, even in the absence of a central authority. Different consensus mechanisms have been developed, each with its own set of advantages and trade-offs.
Some popular consensus mechanisms include:

• Proof of Work (PoW): PoW is the consensus mechanism used in Bitcoin. Miners compete to solve complex mathematical puzzles, and the first miner to find a solution gets to add the next block to the blockchain. PoW is resource-intensive and requires significant computational power, but it is proven to be secure and resistant to attacks.

• Proof of Stake (PoS): PoS is an alternative consensus mechanism that selects validators based on the number of cryptocurrency tokens they hold or "stake." Validators are chosen to create new blocks based on their stake, and the chances of being selected increase with the amount of stake they hold. PoS is more energy efficient than PoW but still ensures network security.

• Delegated Proof of Stake (DPoS): DPoS introduces a voting and delegation system where token holders elect a limited number of representatives, called delegates or block producers, to validate transactions and create new blocks on their behalf. DPoS provides fast transaction confirmations and scalability while maintaining a degree of decentralization.
Consensus mechanisms play a vital role in ensuring the security, efficiency, and scalability of blockchain networks.

Immutable Ledger

Immutability is a key characteristic of blockchain technology. Once a transaction is added to the blockchain, it becomes extremely difficult to alter or delete. This immutability is achieved through the use of cryptographic hash functions, the decentralized nature of the network, and the consensus mechanisms.

The immutability of the blockchain provides several benefits:

• Data Integrity: The immutability ensures that once a transaction is recorded on the blockchain, it cannot be tampered with without detection. This makes blockchain a secure and reliable source of truth for transaction history and other data stored on the ledger.

• Auditing and Transparency: The ability to audit and verify the entire transaction history on the blockchain promotes transparency. Participants can independently verify the integrity and accuracy of the recorded transactions, enhancing trust and reducing the need for intermediaries.

• Dispute Resolution: In cases of disputes or discrepancies, the immutable nature of the blockchain provides an irrefutable and tamper-proof record of transactions.

Smart Contracts

Smart contracts are self-executing contracts with predefined rules and conditions encoded on the blockchain. These contracts automatically execute and enforce the terms of an agreement when specific conditions are met, without the need for intermediaries.

Key aspects of smart contracts are as follows:

• Automation: Smart contracts enable the automation of processes and transactions. Once the predefined conditions are fulfilled, the contract executes automatically, eliminating the need for manual intervention or third-party enforcement.

- **Trust and Security:** Smart contracts are stored on the blockchain, making them transparent, tamper-proof, and resistant to fraud. The execution of smart contracts is based on the consensus rules defined by the blockchain network, ensuring the integrity and trustworthiness of the contract.

- **Efficiency and Cost Reduction:** By removing intermediaries and automating processes, smart contracts can streamline workflows, reduce delays, and lower costs associated with traditional contract execution. The self-executing nature of smart contracts eliminates the need for intermediaries, such as lawyers or escrow services, reducing administrative burdens and costs.

- **Wide Range of Applications:** Smart contracts have a wide range of potential applications beyond financial transactions. They can be used for various purposes, such as supply chain management, decentralized applications (dApps), voting systems, intellectual property management, and more. The versatility of smart contracts opens new possibilities for efficiency and innovation across multiple industries.

Smart contracts operate based on the principle of "if-then" logic. They define the conditions and actions to be taken when those conditions are met. For example, in a supply chain smart contract, if the shipment is delivered and confirmed, the smart contract can automatically trigger the release of payment to the supplier.

While smart contracts offer significant advantages, it's important to note that they are only as reliable as the code they are written in. Bugs or vulnerabilities in the code can lead to unintended consequences or security breaches. Auditing, testing, and proper development practices are essential to ensure the reliability and security of smart contracts.

Smart contracts are a powerful innovation that enhances the capabilities of blockchain technology. By enabling automated and trustless execution of agreements, they have the potential to revolutionize various industries, streamline processes, and create new business models.

Types of Blockchains: Public Blockchains, Private Blockchains, Consortium Blockchains

Blockchain technology can be categorized into different types based on their accessibility, permissions, and governance models. The three main types of blockchains are public blockchains, private blockchains, and consortium blockchains.

Public Blockchains

Public blockchains are open and permissionless networks where anyone can participate, validate transactions, and contribute to the consensus process. These blockchains are decentralized and operated by a distributed network of nodes that collectively maintain the blockchain's integrity and security.

Key characteristics of public blockchains include:

- **Accessibility:** Public blockchains are open to anyone, allowing anyone to join the network, validate transactions, and create new blocks. There are no restrictions or barriers to entry, making them inclusive and transparent.

- **Decentralization:** Public blockchains are decentralized, with no central authority controlling the network. Transactions and data are verified by a network of independent nodes, ensuring consensus and trust among participants.

- **Transparency:** Public blockchains provide transparent and auditable transaction histories. Anyone can view the transactions and account balances recorded on the blockchain, enhancing trust and accountability.

- **Security:** Public blockchains employ consensus mechanisms like Proof of Work (PoW) or Proof of Stake (PoS) to ensure security and prevent malicious activities. The decentralized nature of public blockchains makes them more resistant to attacks and censorship.

Examples: Bitcoin, Ethereum, Litecoin.

Public blockchains are ideal for applications where openness, transparency, and trust are crucial. They are commonly used for cryptocurrencies, decentralized applications (dApps), and various public utility projects.

Private Blockchains

Private blockchains, also known as permissioned blockchains, are restricted networks where access and participation are controlled by a single organization or a group of entities. These blockchains are not open to the public, and the consensus process is usually governed by a central authority or a predefined group of participants.

Key characteristics of private blockchains include:

- Restricted Access: Private blockchains have access restrictions, and only authorized participants can join the network. These participants are typically known and vetted entities, such as organizations or consortium members.

- Centralized Governance: Private blockchains often have a centralized governance model, where a single entity or a consortium of entities determines the rules, consensus mechanisms, and access permissions.

- Increased Efficiency: Private blockchains can achieve higher transaction throughput and faster confirmations compared to public blockchains. The restricted network allows for quicker consensus and reduces the computational overhead associated with achieving consensus in public blockchains.

- Enhanced Privacy: Private blockchains provide greater privacy since the participants are known and vetted. The transaction details and data stored on the blockchain may not be visible to the public.

- Examples: Hyperledger Fabric, R3 Corda, Quorum.
  Private blockchains are commonly used by enterprises and organizations that require a higher degree of control, privacy, and scalability. They are suitable for applications like supply chain management, interbank transactions, and private financial systems.

Consortium Blockchains

Consortium blockchains, also known as federated blockchains, are a hybrid model that combines elements of both public and private blockchains. In consortium blockchains, a group of organizations or entities collectively controls the network, allowing for a more decentralized governance structure compared to private blockchains.

Key characteristics of consortium blockchains include:

- **Controlled Membership:** Consortium blockchains have a predefined set of trusted participants who form a consortium. These participants maintain the network and validate transactions, ensuring a higher level of decentralization compared to private blockchains.

- **Shared Governance:** In consortium blockchains, the consortium members collectively determine the consensus mechanisms, network rules, and access permissions. Decisions regarding the blockchain's governance are made by consensus among the consortium members.

- **Selective Transparency:** Consortium blockchains provide selective transparency, allowing only consortium members to view and access certain sensitive data. This provides a balance between privacy and transparency requirements.

- **Examples:** IBM Blockchain Platform, Corda Network, MultiChain.

Consortium blockchains are well-suited for industries and use cases that involve multiple stakeholders collaborating on a shared network. They are often used in sectors like healthcare, supply chain management, and finance, where trust and cooperation among known entities are crucial.
Each type of blockchain has its own strengths and use cases, and the choice of blockchain type depends on the specific requirements of the application or organization. Understanding these different types of blockchains can help in selecting the most appropriate blockchain solution for a particular use case.

Blockchain Use Cases

Blockchain technology has the potential to revolutionize various industries and transform traditional processes. In this section, we will explore some of the prominent use cases of blockchain technology across different sectors.

1. Financial Services: Blockchain has significant implications for the financial industry, enabling faster, secure, and cost-effective transactions. It can streamline cross-border payments, remittances, and reduce settlement times. Blockchain-based cryptocurrencies, such as Bitcoin and stablecoins, provide alternative forms of digital currencies and decentralized financial systems.

2. Supply Chain Management: Blockchain can enhance transparency and traceability in supply chains. By recording every transaction and movement of goods on the blockchain, stakeholders can verify the origin, authenticity, and quality of products. This is particularly useful in industries such as food and pharmaceuticals, where traceability and quality control are crucial.

3. Healthcare: Blockchain technology can improve healthcare data management, interoperability, and patient privacy. It allows secure storage and sharing of medical records, ensuring data integrity and consent-based access. Blockchain can also facilitate the development of personalized medicine and support clinical research through secure data sharing and collaboration.

4. Identity Management: Blockchain offers a decentralized and tamper-proof system for managing digital identities. It can provide individuals with control over their personal data, reducing the risk of identity theft and fraud. Blockchain-based identity systems can streamline processes like KYC (Know Your Customer) verification, secure voting systems, and digital credentials.

5. Intellectual Property: Blockchain can revolutionize intellectual property management by providing a secure and transparent platform for copyright registration, licensing, and digital rights management. It can protect creators' rights, prevent infringement, and enable fair and transparent distribution of royalties.

6. Energy and Sustainability: Blockchain can enable peer-to-peer energy trading, optimizing energy distribution and reducing reliance on centralized energy providers. It can also facilitate the tracking and verification of renewable energy generation, carbon credits, and sustainability initiatives.

7. Government Services: Blockchain has the potential to improve government services by enhancing transparency, reducing bureaucracy, and preventing corruption. It can be used for secure voting systems, public record keeping, land registration, and digital identity management.

These are just a few examples of how blockchain technology can be applied across various industries. The decentralized and secure nature of blockchain offers opportunities for innovation, efficiency, and trust in many sectors. As the technology continues to evolve, we can expect to see more innovative use cases emerge.

Chapter 3:
Getting Started with Cryptocurrencies

What are Cryptocurrencies?

Cryptocurrencies are digital or virtual currencies that utilize cryptographic techniques to secure and verify transactions. Unlike traditional forms of currency issued by central banks, cryptocurrencies operate on decentralized networks, such as blockchain, that enable peer-to-peer transactions without the need for intermediaries.

Here are key points to understand about cryptocurrencies:

1. Digital Currency: Cryptocurrencies exist solely in digital form and are not physically tangible like traditional cash or coins. They are represented by digital tokens or units of value stored on a digital ledger.

2. Decentralization: Cryptocurrencies are typically decentralized, meaning they are not controlled by any central authority, government, or financial institution. Instead, they operate on a network of computers, known as nodes, that collectively maintain and secure the network.

3. Cryptography: Cryptocurrencies employ cryptographic techniques to secure transactions and control the creation of new units. Encryption algorithms ensure the confidentiality and integrity of transactions, while digital signatures verify the authenticity of transactions and ownership of cryptocurrency units.

4. Blockchain Technology: Most cryptocurrencies are built on blockchain technology, which is a distributed ledger that records all transactions across a network of computers. The blockchain serves as a transparent and immutable record of every transaction, enhancing security and preventing fraud.

5. Limited Supply: Many cryptocurrencies have a finite supply, meaning there is a predetermined maximum number of units that can ever exist. This scarcity contributes to their value and can help protect against inflation.

6. Peer-to-Peer Transactions: Cryptocurrencies enable direct peer-to-peer transactions without the need for intermediaries, such as banks or payment processors. This allows for faster, more efficient, and potentially lower-cost transactions.

7. Diverse Use Cases: Cryptocurrencies have evolved beyond being just digital currencies. They can also represent ownership in assets, serve as utility tokens for accessing decentralized applications (dApps), or facilitate smart contracts—self-executing contracts with predefined rules and conditions.

Examples of well-known cryptocurrencies include Bitcoin (BTC), Ethereum (ETH), Ripple (XRP), and Litecoin (LTC). Each cryptocurrency operates on its own set of principles, features, and use cases, contributing to the overall diversity within the crypto ecosystem.

Understanding the nature of cryptocurrencies is crucial as you navigate the world of digital assets. It enables you to comprehend their unique properties, benefits, and potential risks associated with their use, investment, and adoption.

Blockchain Technology

Blockchain technology serves as the foundation for cryptocurrencies and is a critical component of their decentralized nature and security. In this section, we will explore the basics of blockchain technology and its key characteristics.

1. Decentralization: At its core, blockchain technology is designed to be decentralized, meaning there is no central authority or single point of control. Instead, it operates on a network of computers (nodes) that collectively maintain and validate the blockchain.

2. Distributed Ledger: A blockchain is a type of distributed ledger that records all transactions across the network. Each transaction, known as a block, is cryptographically linked to the previous block, forming a chain. This chain of blocks creates an immutable record of all transactions, ensuring transparency and preventing tampering.

3. Consensus Mechanisms: Blockchain networks rely on consensus mechanisms to reach an agreement on the validity of transactions and maintain the integrity of the blockchain. Different consensus mechanisms, such as Proof of Work (PoW) or Proof of Stake (PoS), ensure that the majority of nodes agree on the state of the blockchain.

4. **Security through Cryptography:** Blockchain technology utilizes cryptographic techniques to secure transactions and protect the integrity of the data. Transactions on the blockchain are encrypted using public-key cryptography, and digital signatures verify the authenticity and ownership of transactions.

5. **Transparency and Immutability:** Once a transaction is recorded on the blockchain, it becomes a permanent and immutable part of the ledger. This feature ensures transparency, as anyone can verify the transaction history. Modifying or tampering with existing blocks is computationally infeasible due to the cryptographic links between blocks.

6. **Smart Contracts:** Blockchain technology enables the execution of smart contracts, which are self-executing contracts with predefined rules and conditions. Smart contracts automatically execute actions when specified conditions are met, eliminating the need for intermediaries, and increasing efficiency and trust.

7. **Potential Beyond Cryptocurrencies:** While blockchain technology gained prominence through cryptocurrencies, its potential extends beyond digital currencies. It can be applied to various industries and use cases, such as supply chain management, healthcare, finance, voting systems, and more, where transparency, security, and trust are crucial.

By leveraging the unique features of blockchain technology, cryptocurrencies can provide secure, transparent, and decentralized digital transactions. The utilization of distributed ledgers, consensus mechanisms, cryptography, and smart contracts enables a trustless environment where transactions can be verified and executed without the need for intermediaries. Understanding the fundamentals of blockchain technology is essential for comprehending the inner workings of cryptocurrencies and exploring their potential applications in various industries.

Cryptocurrency Wallets

Cryptocurrency wallets are digital tools that allow users to securely store, manage, and interact with their cryptocurrencies. In this section, we will explore the different types of cryptocurrency wallets and the importance of wallet security.

1. Software Wallets: Software wallets are applications or software programs that can be installed on computers, smartphones, or tablets. They provide a convenient way to access and manage cryptocurrencies. Software wallets can be further categorized into:

• Desktop Wallets: Installed on a personal computer or laptop, desktop wallets provide users with full control over their cryptocurrency holdings. They are typically more secure than online wallets as they store private keys locally on the user's device.

• Mobile Wallets: Mobile wallets are designed for smartphones and offer the flexibility of managing cryptocurrencies on the go. They are user-friendly and provide a convenient way to send and receive payments using QR codes.

2. Hardware Wallets: Hardware wallets are physical devices specifically designed for securely storing cryptocurrencies. They offer the highest level of security by keeping private keys offline, away from potential online threats. Hardware wallets are connected to a computer or smartphone when transactions need to be signed, ensuring a secure and isolated environment for key management.

3. Online Wallets: Online wallets, also known as web wallets or cloud wallets, are web-based wallets that are accessible through a web browser. They are convenient to use as they allow users to access their cryptocurrencies from any device with an internet connection. However, online wallets carry some level of risk as the private keys are stored on the online platform, making them vulnerable to hacking or theft.

4. Paper Wallets: Paper wallets involve printing out the public and private keys on a physical piece of paper. They offer an offline storage solution, making them highly secure. However, caution must be exercised to ensure the paper wallet is stored in a safe and protected environment to prevent physical damage or loss.

5. Custodial Wallets: Custodial wallets are provided by third-party platforms or exchanges that hold users' cryptocurrencies on their behalf. While they offer convenience and easy access, users must trust the custodial service to secure their funds properly.

It's crucial to prioritize wallet security to protect your cryptocurrencies from unauthorized access or theft. Here are some essential security measures:
• **Strong Passwords:** Use strong, unique passwords for your wallets and avoid reusing them across different platforms.
• **Two-Factor Authentication (2FA):** Enable 2FA for an additional layer of security, requiring a verification code in addition to your password.
• **Backup and Recovery:** Regularly backup your wallet's private keys or recovery phrases and store them in secure offline locations.
• **Keep Software Updated:** Keep your wallet software up to date to ensure you have the latest security patches and enhancements.
• **Exercise Caution:** Be vigilant against phishing attempts, malware, and suspicious websites or applications that may compromise your wallet's security.
By understanding the different types of cryptocurrency wallets and implementing proper security measures, you can effectively manage and safeguard your cryptocurrencies, ensuring a secure and reliable storage solution.

Cryptocurrency Transactions

Cryptocurrency transactions are the backbone of the digital currency ecosystem, enabling users to send, receive, and manage their cryptocurrency holdings. In this section, we will explore the mechanics of cryptocurrency transactions and the key concepts associated with them.

1. Wallet Addresses: To initiate a cryptocurrency transaction, users need to have a wallet address. A wallet address is a unique alphanumeric string that serves as the destination for the cryptocurrency being sent. Wallet addresses are generated using cryptographic techniques and are associated with the user's public key.

2. Transaction Signatures: Cryptocurrency transactions require digital signatures to verify the authenticity of the transaction and prove ownership of the cryptocurrency being sent. Digital signatures are created using the user's private key and provide cryptographic proof that the transaction was authorized by the owner of the wallet.

3. Transaction Verification: Once a transaction is initiated, it needs to be verified and added to the blockchain. This process varies depending on the consensus mechanism used by the specific cryptocurrency network. In Proof of Work (PoW) systems, miners compete to solve complex mathematical puzzles to validate transactions. In Proof of Stake (PoS) systems, validators are selected based on their stake in the network to confirm transactions.

4. Transaction Confirmation: After a transaction is verified, it needs to be confirmed by the network. Confirmation refers to the process of including the transaction in a block, which is then added to the blockchain. The number of confirmations required can vary depending on the cryptocurrency network and the level of security desired. Each confirmation increases the level of trust in the transaction's validity.

5. Transaction Fees: Cryptocurrency transactions may require the payment of transaction fees. These fees are paid to incentivize miners or validators to include the transaction in the blockchain. The fee amount depends on factors such as network congestion, transaction size, and the urgency of the transaction. Higher fees can prioritize the transaction for faster confirmation.

6. Transaction Time: The time it takes for a cryptocurrency transaction to be confirmed and added to the blockchain can vary. Factors such as network congestion, transaction fees, and the consensus mechanism employed by the cryptocurrency network can influence transaction times. Some cryptocurrencies offer faster confirmation times, while others may require more time for security reasons.

7. Scalability Challenges: As cryptocurrency networks gain popularity and transaction volumes increase, scalability becomes a significant challenge. The capacity of blockchain networks to handle a large number of transactions per second can impact transaction speeds and fees.

Various scalability solutions, such as off-chain transactions and layer-two protocols, are being developed to address these challenges.

Understanding the mechanics of cryptocurrency transactions allows users to effectively navigate the digital currency ecosystem. By grasping concepts like wallet addresses, transaction signatures, verification, confirmation, fees, and transaction times, users can make informed decisions when sending or receiving cryptocurrencies and ensure secure and reliable transactions.

Getting Started: Choosing and Acquiring Cryptocurrencies

Once we have a solid understanding of cryptocurrencies, we will move on to the practical aspects of getting started.

Selecting Cryptocurrencies

Choosing the right cryptocurrencies to invest in or utilize requires careful consideration of various factors. In this section, we will explore key aspects to consider when selecting cryptocurrencies, including project fundamentals, market dynamics, and risk assessment.

1. Project Fundamentals: Assessing the fundamentals of a cryptocurrency project is crucial in determining its potential for long-term success. Consider the following:
• Purpose and Use Case: Understand the purpose and utility of the cryptocurrency. Does it aim to solve a real-world problem or provide value in a specific industry? Evaluate its potential for adoption and scalability.
• Technology and Innovation: Examine the underlying technology powering the cryptocurrency. Does it offer unique features or improvements over existing solutions? Consider factors like scalability, security, privacy, and smart contract capabilities.
• Development Team: Evaluate the team behind the cryptocurrency project. Assess their expertise, experience, and track record. Look for transparency, community engagement, and the presence of a strong development roadmap.

2. Market Dynamics: Analyzing the market dynamics surrounding a cryptocurrency is essential to understand its potential growth and volatility.

Consider the following:
• **Market Capitalization and Liquidity:** Assess the cryptocurrency's market capitalization, which represents the total value of all coins in circulation. Higher market capitalization generally indicates a more established and liquid cryptocurrency, making it easier to buy, sell, and trade.
• **Trading Volume and Exchange Listings:** Evaluate the trading volume of the cryptocurrency on various exchanges. Higher trading volume suggests increased market interest and liquidity. Additionally, consider the availability of the cryptocurrency on reputable and regulated exchanges.
• **Market Trends and Sentiment:** Stay informed about market trends, news, and sentiment surrounding the cryptocurrency. Monitor the community's perception, media coverage, and regulatory developments that may impact the cryptocurrency's value and adoption.

3. Risk Assessment: Assessing the risks associated with a cryptocurrency investment is crucial for informed decision-making.

Consider the following:
• **Volatility:** Cryptocurrencies are known for their price volatility. Understand the level of volatility associated with a particular cryptocurrency and assess your risk tolerance accordingly.
• **Regulatory Environment:** Examine the regulatory landscape surrounding cryptocurrencies in your jurisdiction. Understand the potential legal and regulatory risks associated with investing in specific cryptocurrencies.
• **Security:** Evaluate the security measures implemented by the cryptocurrency project and associated wallets or exchanges. Consider factors such as past security incidents, the use of encryption, and the availability of insurance or compensation mechanisms.
• **Market Competition:** Assess the competitive landscape of the cryptocurrency. Consider the presence of similar projects, market share, and potential challenges in gaining adoption and differentiation.

It's important to conduct thorough research, seek expert opinions, and diversify your cryptocurrency portfolio to mitigate risks. Additionally, consider consulting with a financial advisor or knowledgeable individuals in the cryptocurrency space to make informed decisions based on your financial goals, risk appetite, and investment horizon.

Exchanges and Trading Platforms

Exchanges and trading platforms play a crucial role in facilitating the buying, selling, and trading of cryptocurrencies. When selecting an exchange or trading platform, it's important to consider factors such as security, liquidity, fees, supported cryptocurrencies, user experience, and regulatory compliance. Here are key points to understand:

1. Security: Security should be a top priority when choosing an exchange or trading platform. Look for platforms that implement robust security measures, such as two-factor authentication (2FA), cold storage for funds, encryption, and regular security audits. Research the platform's track record regarding past security incidents or hacks.

2. Liquidity: Liquidity refers to the ability to buy or sell a cryptocurrency quickly and at a fair price. Opt for exchanges with high trading volumes and a wide range of supported cryptocurrencies, as this indicates greater liquidity. Higher liquidity makes it easier to execute trades and reduces the risk of slippage.

3. Fees: Exchanges and trading platforms charge various types of fees, including transaction fees, deposit/withdrawal fees, and trading fees. Compare fee structures among different platforms to find the most cost-effective option. However, be cautious of platforms with exceptionally low fees, as they may compromise on security or provide inferior services.

4. Supported Cryptocurrencies: Check which cryptocurrencies are supported by the exchange or trading platform. Ensure that the platform offers the cryptocurrencies you wish to trade or invest in. Additionally, consider the availability of trading pairs, as it allows for greater flexibility in executing trades.

5. User Experience: A user-friendly interface and intuitive trading platform can greatly enhance your trading experience. Look for platforms that offer easy navigation, clear charts and graphs, order book information, and advanced trading features such as stop-loss and limit orders. A responsive customer support team can also be beneficial in case of any issues or inquiries.

6. Regulatory Compliance: Verify that the exchange or trading platform adheres to relevant regulations and operates in compliance with Know Your Customer (KYC) and Anti-Money Laundering (AML) requirements. Regulatory compliance provides an added layer of security and legitimacy to the platform.

7. Reputation and Reviews: Research the reputation and user reviews of the exchange or trading platform. Look for platforms with positive feedback, a strong track record, and a long-standing presence in the cryptocurrency community. User reviews and feedback can provide insights into the platform's reliability, customer support, and overall user experience.

It's advisable to start with reputable and well-established exchanges and trading platforms. However, keep in mind that different platforms cater to different types of traders and investors. Some platforms offer advanced trading features for experienced traders, while others focus on simplicity and ease of use for beginners. Consider your trading needs, preferences, and level of experience when choosing an exchange or trading platform.
Remember to exercise caution and perform due diligence before depositing funds or trading on any platform. Keep your funds secure by using strong passwords, enabling 2FA, and considering the use of hardware wallets for long-term storage of cryptocurrencies.

Managing Risks in Cryptocurrency Investments

Investing in cryptocurrencies carries certain risks, and it's essential to manage them effectively to safeguard your investment. In this section, we will explore key strategies and considerations for managing risks in cryptocurrency investments.

1. Diversification: Diversifying your cryptocurrency portfolio is a fundamental risk management strategy. Instead of investing all your funds into a single cryptocurrency, spread your investments across different cryptocurrencies with varying risk profiles.

This helps mitigate the impact of volatility or potential setbacks in any one cryptocurrency.

2. Research and Due Diligence: Thoroughly research and conduct due diligence on the cryptocurrencies you plan to invest in. Evaluate their underlying technology, development team, use case, market demand, and competitive landscape. Stay updated with relevant news, regulatory developments, and market trends that can impact the value of your investments.

3. Risk Assessment and Risk Appetite: Assess your risk appetite and understand the risks associated with different cryptocurrencies. Consider factors such as price volatility, market liquidity, regulatory risks, and technological vulnerabilities. Align your investment decisions with your risk tolerance and long-term financial goals.

4. Dollar-Cost Averaging (DCA): DCA is an investment strategy where you regularly invest a fixed amount of money into cryptocurrencies at predetermined intervals, regardless of the market price. This approach reduces the impact of short-term price fluctuations and allows you to accumulate cryptocurrencies over time at an average cost.

5. Setting Realistic Expectations: Cryptocurrency markets can be highly volatile, and prices can fluctuate dramatically. Set realistic expectations for your investment returns and be prepared for potential market downturns. Avoid falling for hype or making impulsive investment decisions based on short-term price movements.

6. Secure Storage: Properly secure your cryptocurrencies by using reputable and secure wallets. Hardware wallets, such as Ledger or Trezor, offer offline storage and enhanced security for long-term holdings. Ensure you have backup measures in place to protect your wallet's private keys or recovery phrases.

7. Regularly Review and Monitor: Continuously review and monitor your cryptocurrency investments. Stay informed about market developments, project updates, and changes in the regulatory landscape. Regularly reassess your investment strategy and make adjustments as needed to align with changing market conditions or personal circumstances.

8. Educate Yourself: Enhance your knowledge and understanding of cryptocurrencies through education and research. Stay informed about new projects, emerging technologies, and investment strategies. This knowledge empowers you to make informed decisions and navigate the cryptocurrency market with confidence.

9. Seek Professional Advice: Consider consulting with a financial advisor or cryptocurrency expert who can provide personalized guidance based on your specific investment goals and risk tolerance. Professional advice can help you navigate complex investment strategies and make informed decisions.

Remember that investing in cryptocurrencies involves inherent risks, and the cryptocurrency market can be highly volatile. Only invest funds that you can afford to lose and be prepared for the possibility of losses. By implementing risk management strategies, conducting thorough research, staying informed, and managing your investments prudently, you can minimize risks and increase the likelihood of achieving your investment objectives.

Securing Your Cryptocurrency Investments

Securing your cryptocurrency investments is of utmost importance to protect your digital assets from theft, fraud, or unauthorized access. In this section, we will explore key measures and best practices for securing your cryptocurrency holdings.

1. Use Strong and Unique Passwords: Create strong, complex passwords for your cryptocurrency wallets, exchanges, and other accounts related to your investments. Use a combination of uppercase and lowercase letters, numbers, and special characters. Avoid reusing passwords across different platforms to prevent potential breaches.

2. Enable Two-Factor Authentication (2FA): Enable 2FA wherever possible to add an extra layer of security to your accounts. 2FA requires a secondary verification method, such as a unique code generated by an authentication app or sent to your mobile device, in addition to your password. This significantly reduces the risk of unauthorized access to your accounts.

3. Secure Your Devices: Keep your devices secure by regularly updating the operating system, antivirus software, and other security patches. Be cautious of downloading files or applications from untrusted sources, as they may contain malware or keyloggers that can compromise your security.

4. Use Hardware Wallets: Consider using hardware wallets for storing your cryptocurrencies. Hardware wallets are physical devices that securely store your private keys offline. They provide an extra layer of protection against online threats and are generally considered one of the safest options for long-term storage of cryptocurrencies.

5. Backup Your Wallets: Regularly backup your cryptocurrency wallets to protect against data loss or device failure. Store backups in secure offline locations, such as encrypted external hard drives or offline storage devices. Ensure your backup is encrypted and password-protected for additional security.

6. Be Cautious of Phishing Attempts: Be vigilant against phishing attempts, where attackers try to trick you into revealing sensitive information or accessing malicious websites. Always verify the authenticity of the websites you visit, double-check email sender addresses, and avoid clicking on suspicious links or providing personal information to unknown sources.

7. Research and Use Secure Wallets and Exchanges: Before using a cryptocurrency wallet or exchange, thoroughly research its security features and reputation. Opt for wallets and exchanges with a strong track record of security, robust encryption, and cold storage options. Read user reviews and consider recommendations from trusted sources.

8. Keep Private Keys Offline: Store your private keys offline and in a secure location. Avoid storing private keys on online platforms or cloud storage, as they can be vulnerable to hacking attempts. Offline storage provides an extra layer of protection against online threats.

9. Regularly Monitor Your Accounts: Monitor your cryptocurrency accounts regularly for any suspicious activity. Keep an eye on your transaction history, balances, and login records. Report any unauthorized activity or security breaches to the platform or exchange immediately.

10. Educate Yourself about Scams and Risks: Stay informed about common cryptocurrency scams and risks. Be cautious of investment schemes promising unrealistic returns, unsolicited investment opportunities, or requests for your private keys or sensitive information. Educating yourself about potential risks can help you avoid falling victim to scams.

11. Consider Insurance and Third-Party Security Solutions: Some cryptocurrency platforms and custodians offer insurance or third-party security solutions for added protection. Research and consider these options to further safeguard your investments.

Remember, securing your cryptocurrency investments requires ongoing effort and vigilance. Stay updated on the latest security practices, follow industry news and developments, and adapt your security measures accordingly. By implementing these security measures and being proactive in protecting your cryptocurrencies, you can minimize the risk of theft or unauthorized access and ensure the long-term security of your investments.

Navigating the Crypto Ecosystem

Navigating the cryptocurrency ecosystem involves understanding the various components, participants, and activities that make up this dynamic industry. In this section, we will explore key aspects of the crypto ecosystem, including cryptocurrency exchanges, Initial Coin Offerings (ICOs), decentralized finance (DeFi), and regulatory considerations.

1. Cryptocurrency Exchanges: Cryptocurrency exchanges are platforms where users can buy, sell, and trade cryptocurrencies. They serve as a bridge between traditional fiat currencies and digital assets. Understand the different types of exchanges, their features, fees, and security measures. Choose reputable and regulated exchanges that align with your trading preferences and requirements.

2. Initial Coin Offerings (ICOs): ICOs are a fundraising mechanism used by cryptocurrency projects to raise capital by selling their native tokens. Learn about the ICO process, including conducting thorough due diligence on ICO projects, understanding the whitepapers, team backgrounds, token economics, and project roadmaps. Be aware of the potential risks associated with investing in ICOs, such as regulatory uncertainties and the possibility of scams or unsuccessful projects.

3. Decentralized Finance (DeFi): DeFi refers to a growing sector within the cryptocurrency ecosystem that aims to recreate traditional financial instruments and services using blockchain technology. Explore decentralized exchanges, lending and borrowing platforms, yield farming, and liquidity pools. Understand the risks and rewards associated with DeFi, including smart contract vulnerabilities, market volatility, and potential financial losses.

4. Regulatory Considerations: Cryptocurrencies operate within a regulatory framework that varies across jurisdictions. Stay informed about the legal and regulatory landscape in your country or region. Understand the tax implications of cryptocurrency investments and transactions. Compliance with Know Your Customer (KYC) and Anti-Money Laundering (AML) requirements is increasingly important on regulated platforms.

5. Community Engagement: Engaging with the cryptocurrency community can enhance your understanding and involvement in the ecosystem. Participate in forums, social media groups, and online communities to learn from others, share insights, and stay updated on the latest news and developments. Be cautious of misinformation and exercise critical thinking when evaluating information shared within the community.

6. Market Analysis and Research: Develop skills in market analysis and research to make informed decisions. Study cryptocurrency charts, technical analysis, and fundamental factors that influence the value of cryptocurrencies. Keep track of market trends, news events, and regulatory developments that can impact the overall market sentiment and individual cryptocurrency prices.

7. Education and Continuous Learning: The cryptocurrency ecosystem is continuously evolving. Invest time in educating yourself through reliable sources, online courses, and educational platforms. Stay updated with new technologies, emerging projects, and industry advancements. Continuously improving your knowledge will help you navigate the ever-changing crypto landscape effectively.

8. Risk Management and Investment Strategy: Develop a risk management strategy aligned with your investment goals and risk appetite. Set realistic expectations and diversify your cryptocurrency portfolio to mitigate risks. Regularly review and adjust your investment strategy based on market conditions and personal circumstances.

Remember that the cryptocurrency ecosystem is highly volatile and subject to rapid changes. Exercise caution, conduct thorough research, and consult with experts when needed. By understanding the various components of the crypto ecosystem and staying informed, you can navigate the industry with confidence and make informed decisions in your cryptocurrency journey.

Chapter 4:
Essential Tools and Resources for Cryptocurrency Beginners

Cryptocurrency Wallets

Cryptocurrency wallets are digital tools that allow individuals to securely store, send, and receive their cryptocurrencies. In this section, we will delve into the world of cryptocurrency wallets, discussing their purpose, types, features, and best practices for setting up and securing them.

1. Understanding the Purpose of Cryptocurrency Wallets:

• Cryptocurrency wallets are not physical wallets but digital applications that enable users to interact with their digital assets.
• Wallets store the user's private keys, which are necessary for accessing and managing their cryptocurrencies.
• Wallets provide a user-friendly interface to send and receive cryptocurrencies, monitor balances, and manage transactions.

2. Types of Cryptocurrency Wallets:

• Software Wallets: These wallets come in various forms, such as desktop, mobile, or web-based applications. They offer convenient access to cryptocurrencies but require caution as they may be susceptible to malware or hacking attempts.
• Hardware Wallets: Hardware wallets are physical devices designed specifically for storing private keys offline. They provide enhanced security by isolating the private keys from internet-connected devices.
• Paper Wallets: A paper wallet involves printing the private keys on a physical medium, such as paper. It offers offline storage but requires careful handling to prevent loss or damage.
• Custodial Wallets: Custodial wallets are provided by third-party services, such as cryptocurrency exchanges. Users trust these services to hold and manage their private keys on their behalf.
• Multisig Wallets: Multisig wallets require multiple signatures from different parties to authorize transactions, adding an extra layer of security and control.

3. Features and Considerations:

• Security: Look for wallets that prioritize security features like two-factor authentication (2FA), encryption, and backup options. Ensure that the wallet's development team follows best security practices.

•Supported Cryptocurrencies: Different wallets support varying cryptocurrencies. Check if the wallet supports the cryptocurrencies you plan to store or trade.

• User Experience: Consider wallets with an intuitive user interface and features that align with your needs, such as portfolio tracking, transaction history, and address book functionalities.

• Compatibility: Ensure that the wallet is compatible with your device's operating system or web browser.

• Development Team and Reputation: Research the wallet's development team and its reputation within the cryptocurrency community. Look for wallets with a strong track record and positive user reviews.

4. Setting Up and Securing Your Wallet:

• Generate a Strong Password: Create a unique and strong password to secure your wallet. Avoid using easily guessable passwords or reusing passwords from other accounts.

• Backup Your Wallet: Follow the wallet's backup procedure to securely store a copy of your wallet's private keys or seed phrase. Store the backup in a safe location separate from your primary device.

• Enable Two-Factor Authentication (2FA): Activate 2FA whenever possible to add an extra layer of security to your wallet. It requires a second verification method, such as a unique code generated by an authentication app or sent to your mobile device.

• Keep Your Software Updated: Regularly update your wallet software to ensure you have the latest security patches and improvements.

• Be Cautious of Phishing Attempts: Be vigilant of phishing attempts where attackers try to trick you into revealing your wallet's private keys or sensitive information. Verify the authenticity of websites and double-check email sender addresses.

By understanding the purpose, types, features, and best practices for setting up and securing cryptocurrency wallets, beginners can confidently choose a wallet that suits their needs and take the necessary precautions to protect their digital assets. Remember to thoroughly research and choose reputable wallets to ensure the security and accessibility of your cryptocurrencies.

Portfolio Tracking and Management Tools

Managing a cryptocurrency portfolio effectively is crucial for tracking investments, analyzing performance, and making informed decisions. In this section, we will explore portfolio tracking and management tools that can help cryptocurrency beginners organize and monitor their holdings. Here are some key points to cover:

1. Importance of Portfolio Tracking and Management:

• Portfolio tracking allows you to keep an overview of your cryptocurrency holdings, including the current value, gains, and losses.
• It helps you monitor the performance of individual assets, track investment strategies, and identify trends and patterns.
• Portfolio management tools provide valuable insights for rebalancing your portfolio, adjusting allocations, and optimizing your investment decisions.

2. Features of Portfolio Tracking Tools:

• Real-time Price Tracking: These tools provide up-to-date prices of various cryptocurrencies, enabling you to monitor the value of your portfolio in real-time.
• Transaction History: Portfolio trackers record your transaction history, allowing you to review and analyze past trades, purchases, and sales.
• Gain/Loss Calculation: They automatically calculate the gains or losses on your investments, considering factors like transaction fees and historical prices.
• Performance Analytics: Portfolio management tools offer performance analysis, including metrics such as overall portfolio return, asset allocation, and individual asset performance.

• **Alerts and Notifications:** Some tools offer customizable alerts and notifications for price movements, portfolio value changes, or news updates.
• **Tax Reporting:** Certain portfolio trackers provide features to generate tax reports, simplifying the process of calculating and reporting cryptocurrency gains and losses.

3. Popular Portfolio Tracking and Management Tools:

• **CoinTracking:** CoinTracking is a comprehensive portfolio management platform that offers features like real-time tracking, tax reporting, and customizable analytics.
• **Delta:** Delta provides a user-friendly interface for tracking cryptocurrency portfolios, with features like price alerts, advanced analytics, and portfolio sharing options.
• **Blockfolio:** Blockfolio is a widely used mobile app that offers real-time price tracking, news updates, and portfolio management tools.
• **CoinStats:** CoinStats is a portfolio tracker with a sleek interface, providing features like price alerts, transaction history, and performance analysis.
• **CryptoCompare:** CryptoCompare offers a range of tools, including portfolio tracking, historical data, and market insights for cryptocurrency investors.

4. Best Practices for Portfolio Tracking and Management:

• **Regularly Update Your Holdings:** Keep your portfolio tracker up to date by adding new investments and removing sold or inactive assets.
• **Monitor Asset Allocation:** Analyze the distribution of your investments across different cryptocurrencies and adjust your allocations based on your investment strategy and risk tolerance.
• **Set Realistic Goals:** Define your investment goals and track your progress using the portfolio management tool. Regularly assess if your portfolio aligns with your objectives.

• **Stay Informed:** Utilize the news and research features of portfolio trackers to stay updated on market trends, news events, and regulatory developments.
• **Review and Adjust:** Periodically review your portfolio's performance and make adjustments as needed, considering factors like market conditions, new investment opportunities, and personal circumstances.

By utilizing portfolio tracking and management tools, cryptocurrency beginners can gain a better understanding of their investments, monitor their portfolio's performance, and make informed decisions. Remember to choose a tool that suits your preferences, offers the necessary features, and integrates well with your existing cryptocurrency exchanges or wallets. Regularly reviewing and managing your portfolio will contribute to a more successful and well-informed cryptocurrency investment journey.

Price Tracking and Market Analysis Tools

In the world of cryptocurrencies, staying informed about price movements and market trends is essential for making informed investment decisions. In this section, we will explore price tracking and market analysis tools that can help cryptocurrency beginners stay updated and analyze market conditions effectively.
Here are some key points to cover:

1. Importance of Price Tracking and Market Analysis:

• Price tracking tools provide real-time and historical price data for various cryptocurrencies, allowing users to monitor market movements.
• Market analysis tools offer insights into market trends, trading volumes, and price patterns, helping users make informed investment decisions.
• Tracking prices and analyzing market conditions can assist in identifying entry and exit points, managing risk, and identifying potential investment opportunities.

2. Features of Price Tracking Tools:

• **Real-Time Price Data:** Price tracking tools display real-time prices of cryptocurrencies from various exchanges, allowing users to stay updated with the latest market values.
• **Historical Price Charts:** These tools provide historical price charts, enabling users to analyze price trends over different timeframes, such as hourly, daily, weekly, or monthly.
• **Price Alerts:** Price tracking tools often offer customizable price alerts, notifying users when a specific cryptocurrency reaches a predetermined price level.
• **Multiple Exchanges Integration:** Many tools support integration with multiple cryptocurrency exchanges, consolidating price data from different platforms into a single interface.
• **Watchlists:** Users can create watchlists to monitor specific cryptocurrencies of interest, making it easier to track and compare their performance.

3. Features of Market Analysis Tools:

• **Technical Analysis Indicators:** Market analysis tools often include a range of technical analysis indicators, such as moving averages, relative strength index (RSI), and Bollinger Bands, helping users identify patterns and trends.
• **Volume Analysis:** These tools provide information on trading volumes, allowing users to gauge the level of market activity and liquidity for a particular cryptocurrency.
• **News Aggregators:** Some market analysis tools include news aggregators, gathering relevant news articles and updates from various sources to keep users informed about market events and developments.
• **Social Sentiment Analysis:** Certain tools analyze social media sentiment to provide insights into the overall sentiment surrounding a particular cryptocurrency, helping users gauge market sentiment.

4. Popular Price Tracking and Market Analysis Tools:

• CoinMarketCap: CoinMarketCap is one of the most well-known platforms for tracking cryptocurrency prices, market capitalizations, and basic market data.
• CoinGecko: CoinGecko offers comprehensive market data, including price charts, market capitalizations, and community insights for a wide range of cryptocurrencies.
• TradingView: TradingView is a popular platform that provides advanced charting tools, technical analysis indicators, and a social community for sharing ideas and strategies.
• CryptoCompare: CryptoCompare offers a range of market data, including real-time prices, historical charts, and market news, catering to both beginners and advanced traders.
• CoinCap: CoinCap offers real-time market data, portfolio tracking, and price alerts, providing an intuitive interface for monitoring cryptocurrency prices.

5. Utilizing Price Tracking and Market Analysis Tools:

• Stay Updated: Regularly monitor price tracking tools to stay informed about the latest cryptocurrency prices and market movements.
• Analyze Price Patterns: Use historical price charts and technical analysis indicators to identify patterns and trends, aiding in making informed trading or investment decisions.
• Set Price Alerts: Utilize price alert features to receive notifications when a specific cryptocurrency reaches a desired price level, ensuring you don't miss potential trading opportunities.
•Research Market News: Take advantage of news aggregators and community insights offered by market analysis tools to stay updated with relevant news and events that may impact the cryptocurrency market.
By leveraging price tracking and market analysis tools, cryptocurrency beginners can enhance their understanding.

Security and Risk Management in Cryptocurrency

Security and risk management are paramount when it comes to dealing with cryptocurrencies. In this section, we will explore the importance of security measures and risk management strategies that beginners should consider when engaging in cryptocurrency-related activities. Here are some key points to cover:

1. Understanding the Importance of Security:

• Cryptocurrencies are digital assets that rely on cryptography and decentralized networks, making security a critical concern.
• Protecting your cryptocurrency holdings from theft, fraud, and hacking attempts is essential for maintaining the integrity of your investments.
• Security measures help safeguard your private keys, wallets, and personal information, reducing the risk of unauthorized access or loss.

2. Secure Storage Solutions:

• Hardware Wallets: Consider using hardware wallets, such as Ledger or Trezor, which store private keys offline and provide enhanced security against online threats.
• Software Wallets: If using software wallets, choose reputable options with strong security features, such as encryption, multi-factor authentication, and regular software updates.
• Paper Wallets: Paper wallets involve printing or writing down your private keys and storing them in a safe and secure location away from unauthorized access.

3. Best Security Practices:

• Strong and Unique Passwords: Use complex and unique passwords for your cryptocurrency accounts and wallets. Avoid reusing passwords from other platforms.
• Two-Factor Authentication (2FA): Enable 2FA wherever possible, requiring an additional verification step, such as a unique code generated on your mobile device, to access your accounts.

• Offline Storage and Backups: Keep offline backups of your wallet's private keys or recovery seed phrase in secure locations, such as encrypted external storage devices or safety deposit boxes.

3. Best Security Practices:

• Strong and Unique Passwords: Use complex and unique passwords for your cryptocurrency accounts and wallets. Avoid reusing passwords from other platforms.
• Two-Factor Authentication (2FA): Enable 2FA wherever possible, requiring an additional verification step, such as a unique code generated on your mobile device, to access your accounts.
• Offline Storage and Backups: Keep offline backups of your wallet's private keys or recovery seed phrase in secure locations, such as encrypted external storage devices or safety deposit boxes.
• Regular Software Updates: Keep your wallets and associated software up to date, as updates often include security patches and bug fixes.
• Beware of Phishing Attempts: Be cautious of phishing emails, fake websites, and fraudulent schemes designed to steal your private keys or personal information. Always verify the authenticity of the platforms you interact with.
• Cold Storage: Consider cold storage options, where your private keys are kept offline and away from internet-connected devices, providing an extra layer of security.

4. Risk Management Strategies:

• Diversification: Spread your investments across different cryptocurrencies, industries, or asset classes to reduce the risk of overexposure to a single investment.
• Research and Due Diligence: Thoroughly research cryptocurrencies, projects, and teams before investing. Understand the risks associated with each investment and evaluate their long-term potential.
• Set Realistic Investment Goals: Define your investment goals and risk tolerance. Avoid investing more than you can afford to lose and be prepared for market volatility.
• Stay Informed: Continuously monitor market trends, news, and regulatory developments that may impact the cryptocurrency market. Stay updated with the latest security practices and industry advancements.

• **Start with Small Investments:** Begin with smaller investment amounts to gain experience and understanding of the cryptocurrency market. Gradually increase your investments as you become more comfortable.

5. Seek Professional Advice:

• Consider consulting with financial advisors or experts in the cryptocurrency field to gain insights and guidance on security best practices and risk management strategies.
• **Join Communities and Forums:** Engage with cryptocurrency communities and forums to learn from experienced individuals and share knowledge on security measures and risk management.

By prioritizing security and implementing risk management strategies, beginners can mitigate potential threats and enhance the overall safety of their cryptocurrency investments. Remember, maintaining a proactive approach towards security and risk management is crucial in the dynamic and evolving cryptocurrency landscape.

Taxation and Legal Considerations in Cryptocurrency

As cryptocurrencies gain popularity, it's important for beginners to understand the taxation and legal considerations surrounding their use and investment. In this section, we will explore the key aspects of cryptocurrency taxation and legal obligations that individuals should be aware of.
Here are some key points to cover:

1. Taxation of Cryptocurrency:

• **Taxable Events:** Understand that various cryptocurrency-related activities may trigger taxable events, such as selling or exchanging cryptocurrencies, receiving mining rewards, or earning cryptocurrency through airdrops or staking.
• **Capital Gains Tax:** In many jurisdictions, profits made from selling or exchanging cryptocurrencies may be subject to capital gains tax. The tax rate may vary based on factors such as holding period and your income tax bracket.
• **Record-Keeping:** It's important to maintain detailed records of all cryptocurrency transactions, including dates, transaction amounts, purchase prices, and sale prices. These records will be necessary for accurate tax reporting.

• Tax Reporting: Familiarize yourself with the tax reporting requirements in your jurisdiction. This may involve reporting cryptocurrency transactions on your annual tax return or filing specific cryptocurrency-related tax forms.

2. Legal Considerations:

• Regulatory Landscape: Stay informed about the legal and regulatory framework governing cryptocurrencies in your country or region. Laws and regulations related to cryptocurrencies can vary significantly between jurisdictions.
• Compliance with AML/KYC Regulations: Understand the Anti-Money Laundering (AML) and Know Your Customer (KYC) regulations that may apply to cryptocurrency exchanges and service providers. Complying with these regulations helps prevent illicit activities and ensures a secure environment for cryptocurrency transactions.
• Licensing and Registration: If you plan to operate a cryptocurrency-related business, such as an exchange or a wallet service, research the licensing and registration requirements applicable in your jurisdiction.
• Consumer Protection: Be aware of consumer protection laws and regulations that may apply to cryptocurrency transactions, especially when dealing with exchanges or platforms that hold user funds.

3. Seeking Professional Advice:

• Tax Professionals: Consider consulting with tax professionals or accountants who specialize in cryptocurrency taxation. They can provide guidance on tax obligations, reporting requirements, and any deductions or exemptions that may apply to your situation.
• Legal Experts: If you have specific concerns or questions regarding the legal aspects of cryptocurrencies, seek advice from legal professionals who have expertise in this field.

4. Stay Updated and Compliant:

• Keep Abreast of Changes: Cryptocurrency regulations and tax laws are continuously evolving. Stay updated with the latest developments and changes in the legal landscape to ensure compliance with the applicable laws.

• **Regularly Review Your Tax and Legal Obligations:** As your involvement in cryptocurrencies evolves, periodically review your tax and legal obligations to ensure you are meeting the requirements based on your activities.

Remember, taxation and legal considerations are crucial aspects of the cryptocurrency ecosystem. By understanding and complying with the relevant tax laws and legal obligations, you can minimize potential risks and ensure a responsible and compliant approach to cryptocurrency use and investment.

Security Measures for Online Transactions

When engaging in online transactions involving cryptocurrencies, it's important to prioritize security to protect your assets and personal information. In this section, we will explore various security measures that beginners should consider implementing to safeguard their online transactions.
Here are some key points to cover:

1. Secure Internet Connection:
• **Use a Trusted Network:** Ensure that you are connecting to the internet through a secure and trusted network, preferably a private and password-protected Wi-Fi network. Avoid using public or unsecured networks that may expose your data to potential threats.

2. Secure Communication:

• **Encryption:** Make sure that all your online transactions and communications related to cryptocurrencies are encrypted. Look for websites and platforms that use HTTPS (Hypertext Transfer Protocol Secure) for secure data transmission.
• **Email Security:** Be cautious when sharing sensitive information or cryptocurrency-related details via email. Consider using encrypted email services or secure messaging platforms for confidential communications.

3. Two-Factor Authentication (2FA):

• **Enable 2FA:** Utilize two-factor authentication wherever possible, as it adds an extra layer of security to your online accounts. This typically involves a unique code or verification prompt sent to your mobile device, in addition to your password, when logging in or conducting transactions.

4. Strong Password Management:

• **Use Complex Passwords:** Create strong and unique passwords for your online accounts and cryptocurrency wallets. Avoid using easily guessable information and consider using password management tools to securely store and generate passwords.
• **Password Updates:** Regularly update your passwords and avoid reusing the same password across multiple accounts. This helps mitigate the risk of unauthorized access in case of a data breach.

5. Multi-Signature Wallets:

• **Consider Multi-Sig Wallets:** Multi-signature (multi-sig) wallets require multiple signatures or authorizations to initiate a transaction. This adds an extra layer of security and reduces the risk of unauthorized access to your funds.

6. Keep Software Updated:

• **Operating Systems and Applications:** Regularly update your operating system, web browsers, and cryptocurrency-related applications or wallets. Software updates often include security patches that protect against known vulnerabilities.

7. Beware of Phishing and Malware Attacks:

• **Phishing Awareness:** Be vigilant and cautious of phishing attempts, where malicious actors impersonate legitimate websites or services to trick users into revealing sensitive information. Always double-check URLs, use bookmarks, or manually type web addresses to access your online accounts.

• Anti-Malware Software: Install reputable anti-malware software on your devices to detect and prevent malicious software or malware that may compromise your security.

8. Regularly Back Up Data:

• Backup Wallets and Data: Regularly backup your cryptocurrency wallets, private keys, and important data associated with your online transactions. Store backups in secure locations, such as encrypted external storage devices or offline backups.

9. Exercise Caution with Third-Party Services:

• Be Selective with Exchanges and Wallets: When choosing cryptocurrency exchanges and wallet providers, research their reputation, security features, and user reviews. Stick to trusted and well-established platforms.
• Smart Contract Audits: If utilizing smart contracts, consider having them audited by reputable third-party firms to ensure their security and mitigate potential vulnerabilities.

By implementing these security measures, beginners can significantly enhance the safety of their online transactions involving cryptocurrencies. Remember, maintaining a proactive and security-conscious approach is crucial to protecting your assets and personal information in the digital landscape.

Overcoming Challenges and Pitfalls in Cryptocurrency

While cryptocurrencies offer exciting opportunities, it's important to be aware of the challenges and pitfalls that beginners may encounter. In this section, we will explore common challenges and provide tips for overcoming them.
Here are some key points to cover:

1. Volatility and Market Fluctuations:

• Understand Volatility: Cryptocurrency markets are known for their volatility, with prices often experiencing significant fluctuations. Beprepared for price swings and avoid making impulsive decisions based on short-term market movements.

• **Long-Term Approach:** Consider adopting a long-term investment strategy, focusing on the fundamentals of the projects you invest in rather than short-term price fluctuations.

2. Security Risks and Scams:

• **Educate Yourself:** Learn about common security risks and scams prevalent in the cryptocurrency space, such as phishing attacks, fake initial coin offerings (ICOs), and Ponzi schemes. Stay informed and be cautious when interacting with unfamiliar platforms or individuals.
• **Verify Information:** Double-check the authenticity of websites, social media accounts, and communication channels before sharing personal information or making financial transactions.
• **Due Diligence:** Conduct thorough research on cryptocurrencies, projects, and teams before investing or engaging in transactions. Look for transparency, active development communities, and reputable partnerships.

3. Regulatory and Legal Uncertainty:

• **Stay Informed:** Keep abreast of regulatory developments and legal obligations regarding cryptocurrencies in your jurisdiction. Stay updated with any changes that may affect your activities or investments.
• **Seek Professional Advice:** If unsure about the legal or regulatory landscape, consider consulting legal or tax professionals with expertise in cryptocurrencies.

4. Technical Complexity:

• **Educate Yourself:** Take the time to understand the technical aspects of cryptocurrencies, including blockchain technology, wallets, and transaction processes. Familiarize yourself with common terms and concepts to navigate the cryptocurrency ecosystem more effectively.

• **Utilize Resources:** Make use of educational resources, online tutorials, and reputable sources of information to deepen your knowledge and understanding.

5. Emotional Decision-Making:

• **Manage Emotions:** Emotions can influence investment decisions, leading to impulsive actions. Practice emotional discipline and avoid making decisions based on fear or FOMO (Fear of Missing Out). Set realistic goals, stick to your investment strategy, and avoid making impulsive trades.

6. Lack of Regulation and Investor Protection:

• **Choose Reputable Exchanges:** When using cryptocurrency exchanges, opt for reputable platforms with a proven track record of security, compliance, and user protection. Research user reviews and security features before selecting an exchange.
• **Self-Custody:** Consider self-custody options, such as hardware wallets, to have full control over your private keys and reduce reliance on third-party services.

7. Lack of Adoption and Liquidity:

• **Focus on Established Cryptocurrencies:** In the early stages, prioritize well-established cryptocurrencies with a proven track record and widespread adoption. These tend to have higher liquidity and lower volatility compared to newer or less-known cryptocurrencies.

8. Continuous Learning and Adaptation:

• **Embrace Learning:** Cryptocurrencies and the blockchain ecosystem are continuously evolving. Stay curious, keep learning, and adapt to new developments and technologies to stay ahead in the rapidly changing landscape.

By understanding and preparing for these challenges, beginners can navigate the world of cryptocurrencies more effectively and increase their chances of success. Remember, patience, education, and a long-term perspective are key when entering the dynamic and ever-evolving cryptocurrency market.

Chapter 5:
Storing and Securing Your Cryptocurrency

Introduction to Cryptocurrency Storage

In the world of cryptocurrencies, secure storage is of utmost importance to safeguard your digital assets. Cryptocurrency storage refers to the methods and technologies used to securely store and protect your private keys, which grant access to your funds on the blockchain. In this section, we will provide an introduction to cryptocurrency storage and highlight the need for robust security measures.
Here are the key points to cover:

1. Digital Nature of Cryptocurrencies:

• Unlike traditional currencies or physical assets, cryptocurrencies exist purely in a digital form. They are stored on the blockchain, a decentralized and distributed ledger technology.

2. Private Keys and Access to Funds:

• To control and access your cryptocurrencies, you need a private key—a unique cryptographic code associated with your digital wallet. Private keys are used to sign and authorize transactions on the blockchain.

3. Risks Associated with Cryptocurrency Storage:

• Cryptocurrencies are prone to various risks, including hacking, theft, loss, and user error. Since cryptocurrencies are decentralized and irreversible, it is crucial to ensure the safety and security of your private keys.

4. Hot Storage:

• Hot storage refers to online wallets and other digital storage solutions that are connected to the internet. They provide convenient access to your funds but may be more vulnerable to hacking attempts or malware attacks.

5. Cold Storage:

• Cold storage refers to offline wallets or devices that are not connected to the internet. It provides enhanced security as it significantly reduces the risk of online threats. Cold storage methods include hardware wallets, paper wallets, and offline computer wallets.

6. The Importance of Secure Storage:

• Secure storage is essential to protect your cryptocurrencies from unauthorized access and potential loss. With secure storage practices, you can mitigate the risk of theft, hacking, or accidental loss of your private keys.

7. Balancing Security and Accessibility:

• When choosing a storage solution, it is important to strike a balance between security and accessibility. Cold storage solutions offer higher security but may be less convenient for frequent transactions, whereas hot storage solutions provide convenience but may have higher security risks.

8. Backup and Recovery:

• Implementing regular backups of your wallets and private keys is crucial. In case of device failure, loss, or accidental deletion, having a secure backup ensures that you can recover your funds and regain access to your cryptocurrencies.

9. Ongoing Security Practices:

• Cryptocurrency storage is not a one-time setup but requires continuous security practices. Regularly updating your wallet software, using strong passwords, enabling two-factor authentication (2FA), and staying vigilant against phishing attempts are important ongoing security measures.

Understanding the basics of cryptocurrency storage and the risks involved lays the foundation for implementing robust security measures. By adopting secure storage practices and staying informed about the latest security trends, you can protect your cryptocurrencies and ensure the long-term safety of your digital assets.

Hot Wallets: Online Storage Solutions

Hot wallets are online storage solutions that allow users to store and access their cryptocurrencies conveniently. They are connected to the internet and provide quick and easy access to funds, making them suitable for regular transactions. In this section, we will explore hot wallets in more detail and discuss their features, advantages, and potential security considerations.

Here are the key points to cover:

1. Definition and Functionality:

• Hot wallets are digital wallets that store private keys on internet-connected devices such as computers, smartphones, or web-based platforms.
• They allow users to access their cryptocurrencies anytime, anywhere, as long as they have an internet connection.

2. Types of Hot Wallets:

• Software Wallets: Software wallets are applications installed on computers or mobile devices. They provide a user-friendly interface for managing and accessing cryptocurrencies. Examples include desktop wallets and mobile wallets.
• Web Wallets: Web wallets are online platforms or services that store users' private keys on their behalf. Users can access their funds through a web browser, making them convenient for on-the-go transactions.
• Exchange Wallets: Many cryptocurrency exchanges offer built-in wallets where users can store their funds directly on the exchange platform. These wallets provide quick access to trading features but may have security considerations.

3. Advantages of Hot Wallets:

• **Accessibility:** Hot wallets allow users to access their funds quickly and easily from various devices with an internet connection.
• **Convenience:** They provide a user-friendly interface, making them suitable for beginners and users who frequently engage in cryptocurrency transactions.
• **Integration:** Hot wallets often integrate with other services, such as exchanges or dApps, enabling seamless interactions within the cryptocurrency ecosystem.

4. Security Considerations:

• **Online Security Risks:** Hot wallets, being connected to the internet, are more susceptible to online security risks such as hacking, phishing attacks, or malware.
• **Trust in Third Parties:** With web wallets or exchange wallets, users are entrusting their private keys to third-party platforms, requiring trust in the platform's security practices and reputation.
• **Regular Updates and Security Measures:** It is essential to keep the wallet software and devices up to date with the latest security patches and employ additional security measures like two-factor authentication (2FA) to enhance the wallet's security.

5. Use Cases and Recommendations:

• **Small Amounts and Frequent Transactions:** Hot wallets are suitable for storing smaller amounts of cryptocurrencies intended for regular transactions, such as day-to-day purchases or trading activities.
• **Risk Management:** Consider keeping only a portion of your funds in a hot wallet and store the majority of your holdings in a more secure cold storage solution for long-term storage.

Understanding the features and considerations of hot wallets helps users make informed decisions about their storage options. While hot wallets provide convenience and accessibility, it is important to balance these advantages with proper security measures to mitigate the associated risks.

Regularly updating the wallet software, using strong passwords, and being cautious about online security threats are crucial for maintaining the security of hot wallets.

Cold Wallets: Offline Storage Solutions

Cold wallets, also known as offline storage solutions, offer an extra layer of security for storing cryptocurrencies by keeping the private keys offline and away from potential online threats. In this section, we will explore cold wallets in more detail, discussing their types, advantages, and best practices for using them.

Here are the key points to cover:

1. Definition and Functionality:

• Cold wallets are cryptocurrency wallets that store private keys on offline devices, ensuring that they are not connected to the internet.
• They provide an offline, secure environment for generating and storing private keys, protecting them from potential online attacks.

2. Types of Cold Wallets:

• Hardware Wallets: Hardware wallets are physical devices specifically designed for securely storing private keys. They are often in the form of USB devices and offer robust security features, including encryption and hardware-based key generation.
• Paper Wallets: Paper wallets involve printing out the public and private keys on a physical medium, such as paper. They are offline and provide an additional layer of security if generated and stored properly.
• Offline Computer Wallets: Offline computer wallets, also known as air-gapped wallets, are wallets installed on computers or devices that are permanently disconnected from the internet. They can be used to generate and sign transactions securely.

3. Advantages of Cold Wallets:

• Enhanced Security: Cold wallets provide a higher level of security since the private keys are stored offline, minimizing the risk of online attacks, malware, or hacking.
• Protection against Online Threats: By keeping the private keys offline, cold wallets offer protection against potential online threats, including phishing attempts and malware attacks.
• Control over Private Keys: Cold wallets allow users to have complete control over their private keys, reducing the reliance on third-party platforms and mitigating the risk of unauthorized access.

4. Best Practices for Using Cold Wallets:

• Secure Setup: Follow the recommended setup process provided by the wallet manufacturer and generate private keys in a secure and trusted environment.
• Offline Key Generation: Generate private keys offline to minimize the exposure to potential online threats. Avoid generating private keys on compromised devices or in the presence of an internet connection.
• Backup and Redundancy: Create secure backups of the private keys and store them in multiple physical locations, such as safe deposit boxes or fireproof safes.
• Regular Updates: Keep the firmware or software of hardware wallets up to date by installing the latest security patches released by the manufacturer.
• Verification and Authenticity: Before using a cold wallet, ensure its authenticity and integrity by verifying the manufacturer's official website and checking for tamper-evident packaging.

5. Use Cases and Recommendations:

• Long-Term Storage: Cold wallets are ideal for securely storing large amounts of cryptocurrencies for an extended period, such as long-term investments or significant holdings.

• **Offline Transactions:** Cold wallets can be used to sign transactions offline securely. Users can generate the transaction on an online device, transfer it to the offline wallet for signing, and then broadcast the signed transaction to the network.

Cold wallets offer an additional layer of protection against online threats and are considered one of the most secure methods for storing cryptocurrencies. By following best practices and being diligent about security measures, users can ensure the safety of their private keys and protect their valuable digital assets from potential vulnerabilities.

Best Practices for Secure Storage

When it comes to storing cryptocurrencies securely, implementing best practices is essential to protect your digital assets from potential risks and threats. In this section, we will discuss key recommendations and strategies for secure cryptocurrency storage. By following these best practices, you can minimize the chances of unauthorized access, loss, or theft. Here are the key points to cover:

1. Use Strong Passwords:

• Create unique and complex passwords for your cryptocurrency wallets and accounts. Include a combination of uppercase and lowercase letters, numbers, and special characters. Avoid using easily guessable information such as personal names or birthdays.

2. Enable Two-Factor Authentication (2FA):

• Utilize two-factor authentication whenever possible to add an extra layer of security. 2FA requires you to provide a second verification factor, such as a unique code generated by an authentication app or received via SMS, in addition to your password.

3. Keep Software Up to Date:

• Regularly update the software and firmware of your cryptocurrency wallets, exchanges, and any other related applications. Software updates often include important security patches that address vulnerabilities and strengthen the overall security of the system.

4. Utilize Hardware Wallets:

• Consider using hardware wallets for long-term storage of your cryptocurrencies. Hardware wallets provide offline storage and secure key management, offering a high level of protection against online threats.

5. Implement Multisig Wallets:

• Multisignature (multisig) wallets require multiple signatures to authorize transactions, adding an extra layer of security. By distributing the signing power among multiple private keys, the risk of unauthorized transactions is reduced.

6. Store Backups Securely:

• Regularly backup your wallet data and private keys and store them in secure offline locations. Consider using encrypted external storage devices or offline mediums like paper wallets. Ensure the backups are protected from physical damage, theft, or loss.

7. Be Cautious of Phishing Attempts:

• Beware of phishing attempts that aim to trick you into revealing your private keys or login credentials. Always double-check the website's URL, be cautious of unsolicited emails or messages, and never share sensitive information in response to suspicious requests.

8. Separate Storage for Long-Term and Active Use:

• Consider separating your cryptocurrency holdings into different wallets based on your intended use. Use a hardware wallet or offline storage for long-term investments, while keeping a smaller amount in a hot wallet for active transactions.

9. Regularly Monitor Account Activity:

• Keep a close eye on your cryptocurrency wallet and exchange account activity. Regularly review transaction history and account balances to identify any unauthorized or suspicious activity.

10. Stay Informed and Educated:

• Stay updated on the latest security practices, news, and developments in the cryptocurrency space. Educate yourself about potential risks and new security measures to adapt your storage practices accordingly.

By implementing these best practices and staying vigilant, you can significantly enhance the security of your cryptocurrency storage. Remember that security measures should be regularly reviewed and adjusted as the threat landscape evolves. Taking proactive steps to protect your digital assets is crucial in maintaining the long-term security and integrity of your cryptocurrency holdings.

Securing Your Digital Identity

Securing your digital identity is crucial when engaging in cryptocurrency activities. Your digital identity includes various elements such as personal information, login credentials, and private keys that grant access to your cryptocurrencies. In this section, we will explore important strategies and best practices for safeguarding your digital identity. By following these recommendations, you can mitigate the risk of identity theft, unauthorized access, and potential loss of funds. Here are the key points to cover:

1. Protect Personal Information:

• Be cautious about sharing personal information online, especially on public forums or social media platforms. Limit the disclosure of sensitive information that could be used to target or impersonate you.
• Regularly review your privacy settings on social media and other online platforms to ensure you are sharing information only with trusted individuals or groups.

2. Use Strong and Unique Passwords:

• Create strong, unique passwords for all your online accounts, including cryptocurrency exchanges, wallets, and email accounts. Avoid using easily guessable passwords and consider using a password manager to securely store and generate complex passwords.

3. Enable Two-Factor Authentication (2FA):

• Enable two-factor authentication on all accounts that support it, including cryptocurrency wallets and exchanges. This provides an additional layer of security by requiring a second verification factor, such as a unique code or biometric authentication, along with your password.

4. Secure Your Email Account:

• Your email account is often the gateway to other online accounts. Use a strong password, enable 2FA, and consider using a separate email address for cryptocurrency-related activities to minimize the risk of potential phishing attacks or unauthorized access.

5. Be Cautious of Phishing Attempts:

• Be vigilant about phishing attempts, which often come in the form of emails or messages that appear to be from legitimate sources but aim to trick you into revealing sensitive information. Double-check URLs do not click on suspicious links, and independently verify any requests for personal or financial information.

6. Secure Your Devices:

• Keep your devices secure by using strong passwords or biometric authentication to unlock them. Regularly update your operating system, applications, and antivirus software to ensure you have the latest security patches.

7. Protect Your Private Keys:

• Safeguard your private keys, which grant access to your cryptocurrencies. Use hardware wallets for secure offline storage, create encrypted backups, and avoid storing private keys digitally or in unencrypted formats.

8. Use Encrypted Connections:

• When accessing cryptocurrency-related websites or services, ensure that your connection is encrypted using HTTPS (Hyper Text Transfer Protocol Secure). Look for the padlock icon in the address bar to verify the website's security.

9. Regularly Monitor Account Activity:

• Keep a close eye on your cryptocurrency wallet and exchange account activity. Regularly review transaction history and account balances to quickly detect any unauthorized or suspicious activity.

10. Stay Informed and Educated:

• Stay updated on the latest security practices, emerging threats, and best practices for securing your digital identity. Continuously educate yourself about potential risks and new security measures to adapt your practices accordingly.

Securing your digital identity is a critical aspect of protecting your cryptocurrency investments. By implementing these best practices, remaining vigilant, and staying informed, you can significantly reduce the risk of unauthorized access or loss of funds. Remember, security is an ongoing effort, and regularly reviewing and updating your security measures is essential in maintaining a secure digital identity.

Ongoing Security Practices

Maintaining the security of your cryptocurrency holdings requires ongoing vigilance and adherence to best practices. In this section, we will discuss key ongoing security practices that you should incorporate into your cryptocurrency management routine. By following these recommendations, you can enhance the overall security of your digital assets and minimize the risk of unauthorized access or loss.
Here are the key points to cover:

1. Regularly Update Software and Firmware:

• Stay up to date with the latest software and firmware updates for your cryptocurrency wallets, exchanges, and related applications. These updates often include important security patches that address vulnerabilities and strengthen the overall security of the system.

2. Use Multi-Factor Authentication (MFA) Everywhere:

• Utilize multi-factor authentication (MFA) wherever it is available, beyond just your cryptocurrency accounts. Enable MFA for your email, social media, and other critical online accounts. This adds an extra layer of security by requiring multiple verification factors to access your accounts.

3. Beware of Phishing Attempts:

• Stay cautious of phishing attempts that aim to trick you into revealing sensitive information. Be skeptical of unsolicited emails, messages, or links. Verify the authenticity of websites before entering login credentials or providing any personal information.

4. Regularly Monitor Account Activity:

• Regularly review your cryptocurrency wallet and exchange account activity. Monitor transaction history, balances, and account settings for any signs of unauthorized activity. Report any suspicious transactions or anomalies to the platform's support team immediately.

5. Secure Your Internet Connection:

• Use secure and trusted internet connections when accessing your cryptocurrency accounts. Avoid using public Wi-Fi networks, which may be susceptible to hacking or snooping. Consider using a virtual private network (VPN) for added security.

6. Backup Your Wallets and Private Keys:

• Regularly backup your cryptocurrency wallets and private keys. Store backups in secure offline locations, such as encrypted external storage devices or offline mediums like paper wallets. Test your backups periodically to ensure they can be successfully restored.

7. Educate Yourself on New Threats and Best Practices:

• Stay informed about the latest threats and best practices in cryptocurrency security. Follow reputable sources, forums, and news outlets that provide updates on emerging risks and security measures. Continuously educate yourself to adapt your security practices accordingly.

8. Implement Whitelisting and Address Verification:

• Consider implementing whitelisting for cryptocurrency withdrawals. Whitelisting allows you to specify trusted wallet addresses to which you can send your cryptocurrencies, reducing the risk of accidental or unauthorized transfers.

9. Be Mindful of Publicity:

• Be cautious about publicly sharing your cryptocurrency holdings or transactions. Consider the potential risks associated with revealing your digital wealth and take necessary precautions to protect your privacy and security.

10. Regularly Review Security Settings and Privacy Policies:

• Periodically review the security settings and privacy policies of the cryptocurrency platforms and services you use. Ensure they align with your desired level of security and privacy. Update your settings as needed to maintain optimal security.

By incorporating these ongoing security practices into your cryptocurrency management routine, you can strengthen the security of your digital assets and reduce the likelihood of security breaches or loss. Remember, maintaining security is an ongoing effort, and regular review and adjustment of your security measures are vital in the ever-evolving landscape of cryptocurrency security.

Chapter 6:
Exploring Popular Cryptocurrencies

Bitcoin (BTC)

Bitcoin, the first and most well-known cryptocurrency, has revolutionized the way we perceive and transact with money. In this section, we will provide an introduction to Bitcoin, highlighting its key features, characteristics, and the role it plays in the digital economy.

Introduction to Bitcoin: Bitcoin was introduced in 2009 by an anonymous person or group of individuals using the pseudonym Satoshi Nakamoto. It operates on a decentralized peer-to-peer network known as the blockchain, which enables secure and transparent transactions without the need for intermediaries such as banks or governments.

Key Features and Characteristics of Bitcoin:

• Decentralization: Bitcoin operates on a decentralized network of computers, known as nodes, which collectively maintain the blockchain. This decentralization ensures that no single entity has control over the currency, making it resistant to censorship and manipulation.
• Limited Supply: Bitcoin has a finite supply cap set at 21 million coins. This scarcity is achieved through a process called mining, which involves solving complex mathematical problems to validate and secure transactions on the blockchain. As a result, Bitcoin is often referred to as "digital gold" due to its limited supply and potential to store value.
• Pseudonymity: Bitcoin transactions are pseudonymous, meaning that while transaction details are recorded on the public blockchain, the identities of the individuals involved are not directly linked to their wallet addresses. However, it is important to note that Bitcoin transactions can be traced, and privacy-enhancing techniques can be employed to increase anonymity.
• Security: Bitcoin's security is ensured by cryptographic algorithms and the consensus mechanism known as proof-of-work (PoW). Miners compete to solve complex mathematical puzzles, and the first one to solve it successfully adds a new block to the blockchain. This process makes it computationally expensive to modify transaction history, enhancing the security and immutability of the network.

Bitcoin's Role as a Decentralized Digital Currency and Store of Value: Bitcoin's primary role is that of a decentralized digital currency, allowing individuals to send and receive value directly without relying on intermediaries. It provides a borderless and censorship-resistant medium of exchange that operates on a global scale. Additionally, Bitcoin has gained recognition as a store of value, with some investors perceiving it as a hedge against inflation and economic uncertainty.

An Overview of Bitcoin Mining and its Significance: Bitcoin mining plays a crucial role in the validation and security of transactions. Miners compete to solve complex mathematical puzzles using specialized hardware, contributing computational power to the network. Successful miners are rewarded with newly minted bitcoins and transaction fees. This process not only ensures the integrity of the blockchain but also introduces new bitcoins into circulation. Over time, the mining reward decreases through a pre-programmed halving event, making it increasingly scarce and potentially valuable.

Understanding the fundamentals of Bitcoin is essential for anyone venturing into the world of cryptocurrencies. Bitcoin's innovation lies in its decentralized nature, limited supply, and its ability to facilitate peer-to-peer transactions. By grasping the key features and significance of Bitcoin, you can develop a deeper understanding of the broader cryptocurrency ecosystem and its potential impact on finance and technology.

Ethereum (ETH)

Ethereum is a groundbreaking decentralized platform that extends the capabilities of blockchain technology beyond digital currency transactions. In this section, we will explore Ethereum's role as a decentralized platform, the concept of smart contracts, the native cryptocurrency Ether, and its utility within the Ethereum ecosystem. We will also touch upon Ethereum's scalability challenges and upcoming upgrades, such as Ethereum 2.0.

Introduction to Ethereum and its Role as a Decentralized Platform: Ethereum, introduced in 2015 by Vitalik Buterin, is a decentralized platform that enables the development of decentralized applications (DApps) and the execution of smart contracts. It provides a robust infrastructure for developers to create and deploy blockchain-based applications, transforming the way transactions and agreements are carried out.

The Concept of Smart Contracts and its Impact on DApps: Smart contracts are self-executing agreements with predefined conditions written in code. These contracts automatically execute and enforce the terms of the agreement without the need for intermediaries. Ethereum's introduction of smart contracts revolutionized blockchain technology, enabling the development of DApps across various industries, including finance, supply chain management, gaming, and more. Smart contracts enhance transparency, security, and efficiency by automating complex processes and removing the need for intermediaries.

Ethereum's Native Cryptocurrency, Ether, and its Utility within the Ethereum Ecosystem: Ether (ETH) is the native cryptocurrency of the Ethereum platform. It serves multiple purposes within the ecosystem. Firstly, Ether is used to pay for transaction fees and computational services on the Ethereum network. Miners and validators are rewarded with Ether for their contributions to securing and maintaining the network. Additionally, Ether acts as a medium of exchange within the Ethereum ecosystem, facilitating value transfers and interactions with smart contracts.

An Overview of Ethereum's Scalability and Upcoming Upgrades (Ethereum 2.0): Scalability has been a significant challenge for Ethereum due to limitations in its current architecture. To address this, Ethereum is undergoing a major upgrade known as Ethereum 2.0 or ETH2. This upgrade aims to improve scalability, security, and sustainability through the implementation of a new consensus mechanism called proof-of-stake (PoS) and shard chains. Ethereum 2.0 will allow the network to process a significantly higher number of transactions per second, making it more scalable and efficient.

Ethereum 2.0 will be implemented in multiple phases, gradually transitioning the Ethereum network from the current proof-of-work (PoW) consensus mechanism to PoS. This upgrade is expected to address the scalability challenges and provide a more sustainable and secure infrastructure for decentralized applications and the broader Ethereum ecosystem.

Understanding Ethereum's role as a decentralized platform, the concept of smart contracts, the utility of Ether, and the ongoing developments with Ethereum 2.0 is crucial for anyone interested in exploring the potential of blockchain technology beyond cryptocurrencies. Ethereum's innovative approach has paved the way for a new wave of decentralized applications and has the potential to transform various industries through its advanced features and programmability.

Ripple (XRP)

Ripple is a technology company that aims to revolutionize the global payments industry through its unique approach to digital payments. In this section, we will provide an introduction to Ripple, its role in facilitating fast and low-cost international money transfers, the distinction between Ripple and XRP, and an overview of Ripple's partnerships with financial institutions.

An Introduction to Ripple and its Unique Approach to Digital Payments: Ripple was founded in 2012 with the goal of transforming the traditional financial system by enabling faster, more secure, and cost-effective cross-border transactions. Unlike many other cryptocurrencies, Ripple focuses on providing solutions for banks and financial institutions rather than targeting individual users. Ripple's technology aims to streamline and enhance the efficiency of international payments.

Ripple's Role in Facilitating Fast and Low-Cost International Money Transfers: One of Ripple's primary offerings is the RippleNet network, which enables financial institutions to connect and transact with one another seamlessly. Ripple's technology leverages a consensus algorithm called the XRP Ledger to facilitate near-instantaneous settlement and lower transaction costs compared to traditional systems. This allows for fast and efficient cross-border transactions, reducing the reliance on intermediaries and enabling real-time liquidity.

The Distinction Between Ripple, the Technology Company, and XRP, the Cryptocurrency: It's important to note the distinction between Ripple, the technology company, and XRP, the cryptocurrency. RippleNet, the company's network, operates independently of XRP. While Ripple owns a significant amount of XRP, the cryptocurrency can be used independently of Ripple's technology for various purposes, including transferring value and acting as a bridge currency for cross-border transactions. XRP's utility and value are not solely dependent on Ripple's success but are influenced by broader market factors and adoption.

Overview of Ripple's Partnerships with Financial Institutions and its Impact on the Global Payments Industry: Ripple has formed partnerships with numerous financial institutions worldwide, including banks, payment service providers, and remittance companies. Through these partnerships, Ripple aims to leverage its technology to improve the speed, efficiency, and cost-effectiveness of international money transfers. By offering an alternative to traditional correspondent banking systems, Ripple has the potential to disrupt the global payments industry and make cross-border transactions faster, more transparent, and more accessible.

Ripple's partnerships and collaborations with financial institutions provide validation for its technology and contribute to its growing adoption in the global financial ecosystem. By offering a solution that addresses the inefficiencies and high costs associated with cross-border transactions, Ripple has the potential to reshape the way money moves across borders and create a more connected and inclusive global financial system.

Understanding Ripple's unique approach to digital payments, its focus on facilitating fast and low-cost international money transfers, and the distinction between Ripple and XRP is essential for grasping the impact Ripple can have on the global payments industry. As the adoption of Ripple's technology continues to grow and more financial institutions embrace its solutions, it has the potential to reshape the traditional financial landscape and create a more efficient and accessible global payments infrastructure.

Litecoin (LTC)

Litecoin, often referred to as the "silver" to Bitcoin's "gold," is a popular cryptocurrency that shares many similarities with Bitcoin but offers some distinct features. In this section, we will introduce Litecoin, highlight the key differences between Litecoin and Bitcoin, discuss its position as a popular alternative for everyday transactions, and provide an overview of Litecoin's adoption and community support.

Introduction to Litecoin: Litecoin was created in 2011 by Charlie Lee, a former Google engineer, with the aim of creating a lighter and faster version of Bitcoin. Like Bitcoin, Litecoin operates on a decentralized network and utilizes blockchain technology to enable peer-to-peer transactions. However, Litecoin differentiates itself through certain technical aspects and features.

Key Differences between Litecoin and Bitcoin:

• Transaction Speed: Litecoin offers faster block generation times compared to Bitcoin. While Bitcoin's block time is approximately 10 minutes, Litecoin's block time is around 2.5 minutes. This shorter block time allows for faster transaction confirmations, making Litecoin more suitable for day-to-day transactions.
• Algorithm: Litecoin uses a different hashing algorithm called Scrypt, whereas Bitcoin uses the SHA-256 algorithm. The Scrypt algorithm is considered more memory-intensive, which has the benefit of making Litecoin mining more accessible to a broader range of individuals using consumer-grade hardware.

Litecoin's Position as a Popular Alternative for Everyday Transactions: Due to its faster block generation times and lower transaction fees compared to Bitcoin, Litecoin has gained popularity as a cryptocurrency suited for everyday transactions. It is often seen as a more practical choice for smaller purchases, such as buying goods and services online or transferring funds between individuals. Many merchants and online platforms now accept Litecoin as a payment method alongside Bitcoin and other cryptocurrencies.

An Overview of Litecoin's Adoption and Community Support: Litecoin has a strong and active community of supporters and developers who contribute to its ongoing development and adoption. Over the years, Litecoin has garnered a significant following and has been integrated into various payment systems and cryptocurrency exchanges. It has also gained recognition and support from notable individuals in the cryptocurrency industry. The Litecoin community is actively engaged in promoting the use of Litecoin for everyday transactions and advocating for its broader adoption.

Litecoin's position as a popular alternative to Bitcoin for everyday transactions is driven by its faster transaction speeds, lower fees, and active community support. Its distinct features and focus on usability have made it a preferred choice for individuals seeking a cryptocurrency that can handle everyday transactions efficiently. Whether it's buying goods, transferring funds, or engaging in online commerce, Litecoin offers a viable option for those looking for a practical and accessible digital currency.

Cardano (ADA)

Cardano is a blockchain platform that aims to provide a secure and scalable infrastructure for the development of decentralized applications and the execution of smart contracts. In this section, we will introduce Cardano, explore its unique approach to blockchain governance and consensus algorithm (Ouroboros), discuss the role of its ADA cryptocurrency within the platform's ecosystem, and provide an overview of Cardano's ongoing development and future plans.

Introduction to Cardano: Cardano was founded in 2015 by a team of engineers, mathematicians, and researchers with the goal of creating a blockchain platform that addresses the limitations of existing networks. It places a strong emphasis on sustainability, scalability, and formal verification of its protocols, making it a promising platform for building secure and reliable decentralized applications.

Cardano's Unique Approach to Blockchain Governance and Consensus Algorithm (Ouroboros): One of Cardano's distinguishing features is its approach to blockchain governance. The platform is designed to be highly decentralized, allowing ADA holders to participate in the decision-making process through a voting mechanism. This ensures that the platform evolves in a democratic and transparent manner, considering the input and preferences of the community.

Cardano's consensus algorithm, called Ouroboros, is a proof-of-stake (PoS) protocol that ensures the security and integrity of the network. Ouroboros divides time into epochs and uses a leader selection process to determine who validates the transactions within each epoch. This energy-efficient algorithm enables Cardano to achieve scalability while maintaining security and decentralization.

The Role of Cardano's ADA Cryptocurrency in the Platform's Ecosystem: ADA is the native cryptocurrency of the Cardano platform. It serves multiple purposes within the ecosystem. Firstly, ADA is used for transaction fees and as a means of value transfer within the network. ADA holders can also participate in the platform's governance and decision-making processes by staking their ADA and earning rewards. Furthermore, ADA can be used as a medium of exchange and a store of value.

Overview of Cardano's Ongoing Development and Future Plans: Cardano has a structured development approach based on peer-reviewed research and scientific principles. It follows a series of development phases, including Byron, Shelley, Goguen, Basho, and Voltaire, each introducing new features and capabilities to the platform.

Cardano's ongoing development focuses on enhancing its smart contract functionality, improving interoperability, and expanding its ecosystem through partnerships and collaborations.

In the future, Cardano aims to become a fully decentralized and sustainable platform that supports a wide range of decentralized applications and enables seamless integration with existing financial and economic systems. The platform's long-term vision includes providing solutions for identity management, supply chain tracking, voting systems, and more.

Cardano's commitment to scientific rigor, sustainable governance, and scalability positions it as a promising blockchain platform in the cryptocurrency landscape. Its unique approach to blockchain governance, consensus algorithm, and ongoing development efforts contribute to its potential to address real-world challenges and enable the development of secure and scalable decentralized applications.

Binance Coin (BNB)

Binance Coin (BNB) is the native cryptocurrency of the Binance exchange, one of the largest and most prominent cryptocurrency exchanges globally. In this section, we will introduce Binance Coin, explore its use cases within the Binance ecosystem, discuss its role in the Binance Smart Chain, and provide an overview of Binance's broader ecosystem and its impact on the cryptocurrency industry.

Introduction to Binance Coin: Binance Coin was launched in 2017 as an integral part of the Binance exchange. It operates on the Binance Chain and serves multiple purposes within the Binance ecosystem. Initially, BNB was created as a utility token to facilitate discounted trading fees for users on the Binance exchange. However, it has since expanded its functionality and has become an essential component of the broader Binance ecosystem.

Use Cases of BNB within the Binance Ecosystem: BNB offers various use cases within the Binance ecosystem. Firstly, BNB holders can enjoy fee discounts when trading on the Binance exchange. This provides an incentive for traders to hold and use BNB for their transactions. Additionally, BNB can be used to participate in token sales on the Binance Launchpad, where users can invest in new and promising projects.

BNB holders also have access to special events, promotions, and services on the Binance platform.

Binance Coin's Role in the Binance Smart Chain: Binance Coin plays a crucial role in the Binance Smart Chain (BSC), which is a parallel blockchain developed by Binance. BSC enables the creation of decentralized applications (DApps) and smart contracts, similar to the Ethereum network. BNB serves as the native cryptocurrency within the BSC ecosystem, allowing users to pay for transaction fees, participate in staking, and interact with various DeFi applications built on the BSC.

Potential for DeFi Applications: The Binance Smart Chain has gained significant attention within the decentralized finance (DeFi) space due to its low fees and high transaction throughput. As a result, BNB has become a popular cryptocurrency for various DeFi applications built on the Binance Smart Chain. Users can utilize BNB to participate in yield farming, decentralized exchanges, lending and borrowing protocols, and other innovative DeFi projects within the BSC ecosystem.

Overview of Binance's Broader Ecosystem and its Impact on the Cryptocurrency Industry: Binance has established itself as more than just a cryptocurrency exchange. It has built a comprehensive ecosystem that includes various services and products. Apart from the exchange and Binance Smart Chain, Binance offers features such as Binance Launchpad for token sales, Binance Academy for educational resources, Binance Wallet for secure storage, and Binance Charity Foundation for philanthropic initiatives.

Binance's ecosystem has had a significant impact on the cryptocurrency industry, providing a seamless and comprehensive platform for users to trade, invest, and engage with various blockchain-based services. The integration of BNB within this ecosystem has further enhanced its utility and adoption, making it a valuable asset for users within the Binance community.

Binance Coin's versatile use cases within the Binance ecosystem, its role in the Binance Smart Chain, and Binance's broader ecosystem have contributed to its growing popularity and influence in the cryptocurrency industry. As Binance continues to innovate and expand its ecosystem, BNB is poised to play an important role in shaping the future of cryptocurrency trading, decentralized finance, and blockchain-based services.

Other Prominent Cryptocurrencies

In addition to the well-known cryptocurrencies discussed earlier, there are several other notable cryptocurrencies that have made a significant impact in the cryptocurrency landscape. In this section, we will provide a brief overview of some of these cryptocurrencies, highlighting their unique features, use cases, and significance.

Bitcoin Cash (BCH): Bitcoin Cash emerged in 2017 as a result of a hard fork from the original Bitcoin blockchain. It aimed to address some of Bitcoin's limitations by increasing the block size, thereby enabling faster transactions and lower fees. Bitcoin Cash serves as a peer-to-peer electronic cash system, emphasizing its use for everyday transactions and merchant adoption.

Polkadot (DOT): Polkadot is a multi-chain platform that enables interoperability between different blockchains. Its innovative design allows independent blockchains to connect and share information securely. Polkadot aims to create a scalable and interconnected network of blockchains, facilitating seamless communication and the transfer of assets between different blockchain ecosystems.

Chainlink (LINK): Chainlink is a decentralized oracle network that connects smart contracts with real-world data and external APIs. It acts as a bridge between blockchain platforms and real-world information, enabling smart contracts to interact with real-time data, payment systems, and external APIs. Chainlink's decentralized oracle network enhances the reliability, security, and functionality of smart contracts across various industries.

Stellar (XLM): Stellar is an open-source blockchain platform designed to facilitate fast and low-cost cross-border transactions. It aims to bridge the gap between traditional financial systems and blockchain technology, providing efficient and inclusive financial services globally. Stellar's native cryptocurrency, XLM, serves as a means of transferring value and participating in the platform's ecosystem.

Cardano (ADA): Cardano, introduced earlier, is a blockchain platform that emphasizes security, scalability, and sustainability. Its unique approach to blockchain governance, consensus algorithm, and focus on formal verification make it a promising platform for the development of secure and reliable decentralized applications.

ADA, the native cryptocurrency of Cardano, plays a crucial role in the platform's ecosystem and governance.

These are just a few examples of other prominent cryptocurrencies in the market. Each cryptocurrency has its own unique features, use cases, and value propositions. It's important for beginners to conduct thorough research and due diligence when considering investments or exploring the potential of different cryptocurrencies. Understanding the underlying technology, team, community support, and market dynamics can provide valuable insights into the viability and long-term prospects of these cryptocurrencies in the evolving digital economy.

Chapter 7:
Practical Use Cases and Future Trends

Cryptocurrency as a Payment Method: Merchants and Adoption

Cryptocurrencies have the potential to revolutionize the way we make payments, offering advantages such as fast and secure transactions, reduced fees, and increased privacy. In this section, we will explore the practical use cases of cryptocurrencies as a payment method and discuss the increasing adoption by merchants worldwide.

Cryptocurrency payment adoption has seen significant growth in recent years, with an increasing number of merchants and businesses accepting cryptocurrencies as a form of payment. Major companies such as Microsoft, Overstock, and Shopify have embraced cryptocurrencies, allowing customers to purchase their products and services using digital assets. This adoption has been facilitated by payment processors and gateways that enable merchants to accept cryptocurrencies and convert them into their preferred fiat currency.

One of the key benefits of accepting cryptocurrencies is the ability to facilitate fast and borderless transactions. Cryptocurrency payments can be processed within minutes, regardless of geographical boundaries. This is especially advantageous for businesses operating in the global marketplace, as it eliminates the need for traditional banking intermediaries and reduces transaction costs associated with cross-border payments.

Furthermore, accepting cryptocurrencies can lead to cost savings for merchants. Cryptocurrency transactions typically have lower fees compared to traditional payment methods such as credit cards, which often involve interchange fees and other processing costs. By accepting cryptocurrencies, merchants can pass on these cost savings to customers or reinvest them into their business.

Another important aspect of cryptocurrency payments is enhanced privacy. While transactions on public blockchains are transparent, they are pseudonymous, meaning that personal information is not directly linked to the transaction. This can provide an additional layer of privacy for both merchants and customers compared to traditional payment systems that often require the disclosure of personal information.

To facilitate merchant adoption, various payment processors and crypto payment gateways have emerged. These services enable merchants to accept cryptocurrencies and seamlessly convert them into their preferred fiat currency. They provide user-friendly interfaces, integration options with popular e-commerce platforms, and the ability to manage transactions and track payments.

However, there are challenges to wider cryptocurrency payment adoption that need to be addressed. These include price volatility, regulatory uncertainties, and the need for user-friendly solutions. Price volatility can be mitigated by instant conversion services that allow merchants to convert received cryptocurrencies into stablecoins or fiat currencies immediately. Regulatory frameworks are also evolving to provide clarity and consumer protection, which can boost merchant confidence in accepting cryptocurrencies.

As the adoption of cryptocurrencies continues to grow, it is crucial for merchants to evaluate the benefits and risks associated with accepting cryptocurrencies as a payment method. Conducting proper due diligence, implementing robust security measures, and choosing reliable payment processors are essential steps for merchants considering cryptocurrency adoption.

In conclusion, cryptocurrencies have emerged as a viable payment method with numerous benefits for merchants. The increasing adoption of cryptocurrencies by major companies and the availability of payment processors and gateways are driving the acceptance of digital assets in the business world. As the cryptocurrency ecosystem matures and regulatory frameworks develop, the adoption of cryptocurrencies as a payment method is likely to continue to expand, providing merchants and customers with greater flexibility, efficiency, and security in financial transactions.

Investing in Cryptocurrencies: Strategies and Diversification

Investing in cryptocurrencies has gained significant popularity as more people recognize the potential for substantial returns and diversification of their investment portfolios. However, it's important to approach cryptocurrency investments with a well-defined strategy and an understanding of the inherent risks.

In this section, we will explore various investment strategies and the concept of diversification when investing in cryptocurrencies.

1. Long-Term Holding: One popular strategy in the cryptocurrency space is long-term holding, also known as "HODLING." This strategy involves acquiring cryptocurrencies and holding them for an extended period, typically years, with the belief that their value will appreciate significantly over time. Long-term holding requires patience and a strong conviction in the potential of the chosen cryptocurrencies.

2. Dollar-Cost Averaging (DCA): Dollar-cost averaging is an investment strategy that involves regularly investing a fixed amount of money into cryptocurrencies at predetermined intervals, regardless of the market price. This strategy allows investors to mitigate the impact of short-term price fluctuations and accumulate cryptocurrencies over time at an average cost. DCA is suitable for investors who prefer a disciplined and consistent approach to investing.

3. Active Trading: Active trading involves buying and selling cryptocurrencies based on short-term price movements to generate profits. Traders use various techniques such as technical analysis, chart patterns, and market indicators to make informed trading decisions. Active trading requires a deep understanding of market dynamics, risk management, and the ability to react quickly to market changes. It is considered a more advanced and potentially higher-risk strategy.

4. Portfolio Diversification: Diversification is a fundamental principle of investment that helps reduce risk by spreading investments across different assets. In the context of cryptocurrencies, diversification involves investing in a variety of cryptocurrencies rather than focusing on a single coin. By diversifying your portfolio, you can potentially mitigate the impact of any negative price movements in a particular cryptocurrency and take advantage of opportunities in different segments of the market.

When diversifying a cryptocurrency portfolio, it's important to consider factors such as market capitalization, project fundamentals, team expertise, community support, and market liquidity. Diversification can be achieved by investing in cryptocurrencies from different categories, such as large-cap coins (e.g., Bitcoin, Ethereum), mid-cap coins, and potentially even some smaller-cap or emerging projects.

Additionally, diversifying across different sectors within the cryptocurrency ecosystem, such as DeFi, privacy coins, or utility tokens, can provide exposure to different trends and potential growth areas.

It's essential to conduct thorough research and due diligence before investing in any cryptocurrency. Factors to consider include the project's technology, use case, team, partnerships, regulatory compliance, and overall market sentiment. It's also prudent to stay informed about market trends, news, and regulatory developments that could impact the cryptocurrency market as a whole or specific coins in your portfolio.

Lastly, risk management is crucial when investing in cryptocurrencies. Investing only what you can afford to lose, setting clear investment goals, and diversifying your portfolio are important steps to manage risk effectively.

In conclusion, investing in cryptocurrencies requires careful consideration and adherence to a well-defined investment strategy. Long-term holding, dollar-cost averaging, active trading, and portfolio diversification are some of the strategies that investors can employ. However, it's important to remember that the cryptocurrency market is highly volatile and can be subject to regulatory changes and other external factors. Therefore, conducting thorough research, staying informed, and exercising prudence are key to making informed investment decisions in the cryptocurrency space.

NFTs and Their Impact on the Art and Gaming Industries

Non-Fungible Tokens (NFTs) have emerged as a revolutionary technology that is transforming the art and gaming industries. NFTs allow for the ownership and authentication of unique digital assets, such as artwork, collectibles, and in-game items, using blockchain technology. In this section, we will explore the concept of NFTs and their significant impact on the art and gaming sectors.

1. NFTs in the Art Industry: NFTs have revolutionized the art world by providing a secure and transparent way to prove ownership and authenticity of digital artwork. Artists can tokenize their creations as NFTs, allowing them to retain ownership and control over their work while selling digital copies to collectors. This has opened up new avenues for artists to monetize their digital creations directly, without the need for intermediaries.

NFTs have also introduced a new level of scarcity and provenance in the digital art market. Each NFT represents a unique piece of art, which cannot be duplicated or forged. The blockchain records the ownership history and transaction details, providing a transparent and immutable ledger of ownership. This has brought about a paradigm shift in how art is created, collected, and traded.

2. NFTs in the Gaming Industry: NFTs have had a significant impact on the gaming industry, particularly in the realm of virtual economies and in-game assets. With NFTs, players can truly own their digital assets within a game, such as virtual real estate, characters, weapons, and skins. These assets can be bought, sold, and traded on blockchain-based marketplaces, providing players with real-world value for their in-game achievements and investments.

NFTs also enable interoperability between different games and platforms. Players can transfer their NFT-based assets from one game to another, creating a seamless and interconnected gaming experience. This has opened up possibilities for cross-game collaborations, shared economies, and new gameplay mechanics.

Moreover, NFTs have allowed game developers and content creators to monetize their creations more effectively. By tokenizing and selling unique in-game items or limited-edition collectibles as NFTs, developers can generate additional revenue streams and foster a more vibrant gaming ecosystem.

3. Challenges and Opportunities: While NFTs present exciting opportunities, there are challenges that need to be addressed. Scalability, environmental concerns related to blockchain energy consumption, and the need for user-friendly interfaces are some of the areas that require further development and improvement.

However, the potential impact of NFTs on the art and gaming industries is immense. NFTs have empowered artists, creators, and gamers by providing new ways to express, monetize, and engage with digital assets. The concept of digital ownership has been redefined, and the boundaries between physical and digital art, as well as virtual and real-world economies, are blurring.

As the technology evolves, NFTs have the potential to disrupt traditional models of art ownership, provenance, and distribution. They can create new revenue streams for artists, enhance the gaming experience, and foster vibrant communities.

It will be fascinating to see how NFTs continue to shape the art and gaming industries and pave the way for new possibilities in the digital realm.

Future Developments in Blockchain Technology and DeFi

Blockchain technology and decentralized finance (DeFi) have already made significant advancements, but their journey is far from over. The future holds exciting possibilities for further development and innovation in these areas. In this section, we will explore some of the potential future developments in blockchain technology and DeFi.

1. Scalability Solutions: One of the key challenges facing blockchain technology is scalability. As more users join blockchain networks and the demand for decentralized applications (DApps) increases, scalability becomes crucial. Several scalability solutions are being explored, such as layer-two protocols like the Lightning Network for Bitcoin and state channels for Ethereum. These solutions aim to increase transaction throughput, reduce fees, and improve the overall scalability of blockchain networks.

2. Interoperability: Interoperability is another important area of development in blockchain technology. Currently, most blockchain networks operate in isolation, limiting the flow of assets and information between them. Future developments will focus on enabling seamless interoperability between different blockchains, allowing for the transfer of assets and data across multiple networks. This will foster greater collaboration, increase liquidity, and enhance the overall efficiency of the blockchain ecosystem.

3. Enhanced Privacy and Security: Privacy and security are paramount in the blockchain space. Future developments will focus on improving privacy features to protect user data and transactional information. Advancements in zero-knowledge proofs, ring signatures, and other cryptographic techniques will enable greater privacy on public blockchains. Additionally, enhanced security measures will be implemented to mitigate the risks of hacks, vulnerabilities, and smart contract exploits.

4. Decentralized Identity: Decentralized identity (DID) solutions aim to provide individuals with control over their digital identities and personal data. These solutions leverage blockchain technology to create self-sovereign identities that are secure, verifiable, and portable.

Future developments in decentralized identity will focus on enhancing privacy, usability, and integration with existing systems, paving the way for a more secure and user-centric digital identity ecosystem.

5. Expansion of DeFi: Decentralized finance (DeFi) has emerged as a transformative force in the blockchain space, providing a wide range of financial services without the need for intermediaries. The future of DeFi holds immense potential for further growth and innovation. We can expect to see the development of new DeFi protocols, novel financial instruments, and increased integration with traditional finance. The expansion of DeFi will contribute to greater financial inclusion, liquidity, and accessibility to a broader range of financial services.

6. Regulation and Mainstream Adoption: As blockchain technology and DeFi continue to evolve, regulatory frameworks will play a crucial role in shaping their future. Governments and regulatory bodies are increasingly recognizing the importance of blockchain technology and its potential impact on various sectors. Future developments will focus on establishing clear regulatory guidelines that foster innovation while ensuring consumer protection and market integrity. Mainstream adoption of blockchain technology and DeFi will accelerate as regulatory clarity increases.

In conclusion, the future of blockchain technology and DeFi is full of possibilities. Scalability solutions, interoperability, enhanced privacy and security, decentralized identity, expansion of DeFi, and regulatory developments are some of the areas that will shape the future of these technologies. As they continue to evolve, blockchain technology and DeFi have the potential to revolutionize industries, empower individuals, and create a more inclusive and efficient global financial system.

MG Horizons Editions

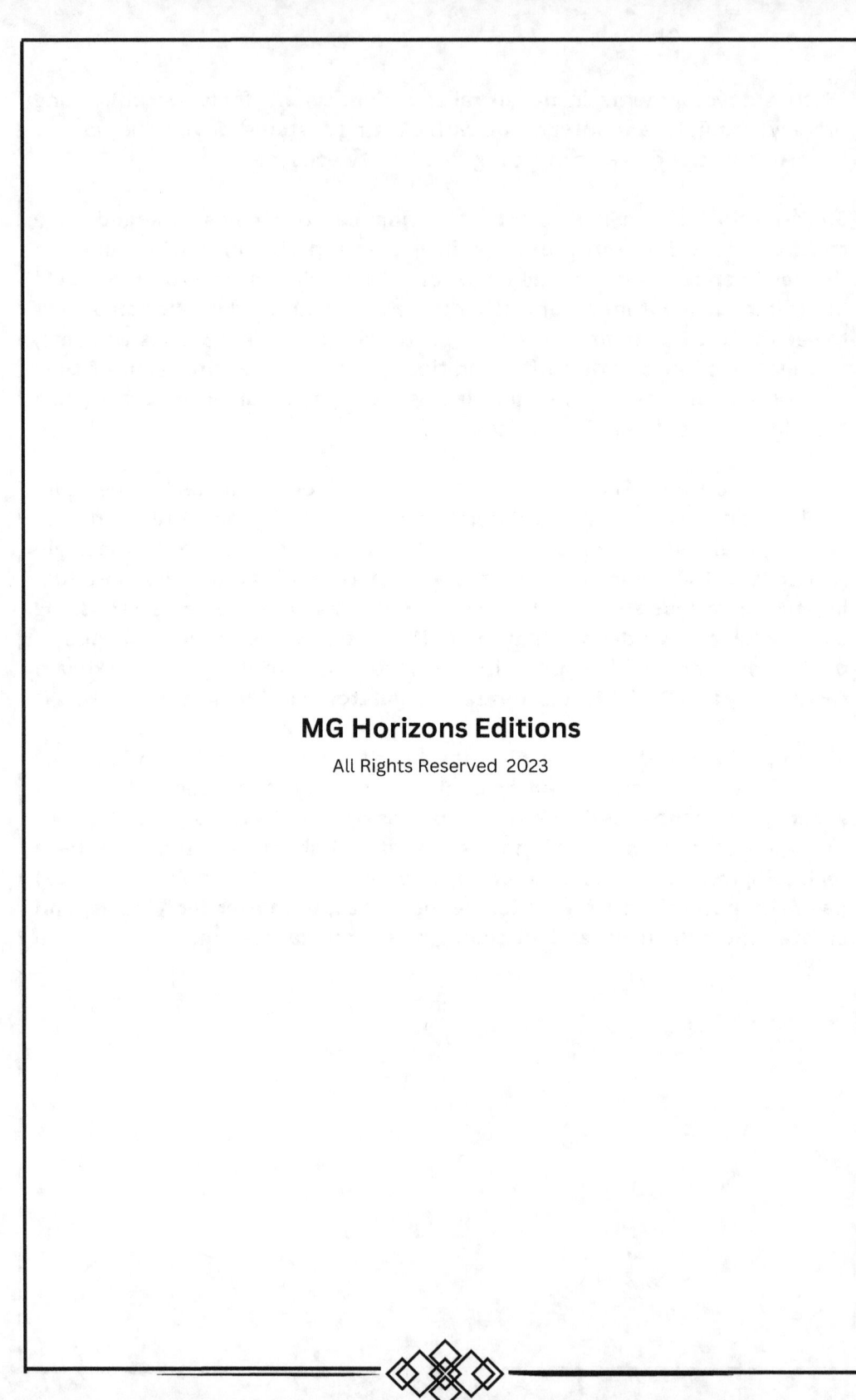